The Psychedelic Path

The Psychedelic Path

An Exploration of Shamanic Plants for Spiritual Awakening

RICHARD L. HAIGHT

Shinkaikan Body, Mind, Spirit LLC

www.richardhaight.net

ISBN 978-0-9992100-4-8

Disclaimer:
Some names and identifying details have been changed to protect the privacy of individuals.

This book is not intended as a substitute for the medical or psychological advice of physicians/psychiatrists. The reader should regularly consult health practitioners in matters relating to physical or mental/emotional health and particularly with respect to any symptoms that may require diagnosis or medical attention.

Published by Shinkaikan Body, Mind, Spirit LLC
 www.richardhaight.net

Shinkaido penned by Osaki Shizen (July 2012)

CONTENTS

Introduction

"I'm a purist," my teacher said. "I don't believe that psychedelics are necessary or even useful on the path of awakening. I feel that it is up to me to awaken on my own." He echoed my personally held belief exactly. We were discussing my upcoming trip to the Amazon, where I was considering partaking in an ayahuasca ceremony with an Achuar shaman.

Although I'd had many visions throughout my life, without aid of psychedelics, and I was an avid meditator, actively dedicated to my path of awakening, I felt undeniably pulled to the ayahuasca experience. I had experienced such a pull many times in my life, and I have learned to trust it deeply; with each one that I followed, there was a great, if not always pleasant, lesson that invariably proved to be a milestone in my life.

My purist ideology and the pull to take ayahuasca were diametrically opposed inner forces, so I took the matter to my mentor in hopes of gaining some clarity on the issue. As my mentor and I were of the same ideology, he said that he was ill-suited to advise me on the decision, but he assured me that he trusted whatever I chose. Somehow that helped me, for I was still at a somewhat insecure place in my awakening process. My mentor, sensing my insecurity, told me plainly, "Trust yourself, for in every interaction I have ever had with you, it was clear that you have powerful inner guidance." Hearing that, I decided my course, and a few months later I was lying at the forest edge of an Achuar village in the midst of a harrowing vision.

After that trip I spent the better part of a decade exploring what I had received from my Amazon experience before I felt the draw to explore psychedelics further. By that time I was an instructor of meditation, autonomic therapy, and Japanese traditional martial arts.

My meditation students and I were discussing the ayahuasca experience when a student asked my opinion about psilocybin mushrooms and whether I thought they could be used as a tool for awakening. As I'd only had one psychedelic experience up to that point in my life, and as mushrooms are distinct from ayahuasca, I had no opinion to offer.

I have had numerous visions throughout my life, and as a result of them I have discovered many powerful tools of awakening: unconditioned meditation, autonomic releasing, and specialized internal martial arts training. Surely there were many other effective tools, I thought. Could psilocybin mushrooms prove themselves to be another spoke on the wheel of awakening leading to the hub—Oneness?

To my surprise during my drive home, while considering my student's question, I felt a strong pull to try the mushroom. This pull led to an exploration of psychedelics that began with psilocybin mushrooms and ended with the pound-for-pound most powerful of naturally occurring psychedelics known to the modern world, *Salvia divinorum*, "the diviner's sage."

Psychedelics are both hyped and denigrated by differing factions within the awakening community. The more traditionally inclined tend to look negatively upon the use of psychedelics, whereas the more open-minded individuals tend to hail psychedelics. The chasm between these two groups is quite vast. I was caught between these two worlds by my "purist" ideology and the opposing pull to explore these substances.

Heading into this experiment, I hoped that my experiences could somehow begin to bridge the gap between these two groups. My policy is to follow the pull wherever it leads me, come what may. To do otherwise would mar integrity and halt my awakening process. My subsequent experiment with psychedelics involved 12 trips over a two-year period.

In this work I intend to walk you through my approach to psychedelics and to detail my key journeys and what I learned from them. I will also share with you the most current scientific information available on these substances and their potential medical uses, legal statuses, safety profiles, and methods for usage.

Although I thoroughly researched the available literature on these substances before taking them myself, I ultimately followed my inner guidance regarding method, which resulted in an approach that is somewhat distinct from what is typically recommended. I share it with you in case you, too, might find it useful.

One of my intentions with this book is to help the reader determine whether psychedelics are appropriate for them. In my opinion, psychedelics are not for everyone. Listening to enthusiastic proponents of psychedelics, we might assume that psychedelic trips are inherently pleasant. To dispel such notions, I have detailed many unpleasant, unflattering, and painful experiences as accurately as possible. If reading this book offends sensibilities, psychedelics may not be for you.

Beyond helping people to decide whether to include psychedelics as part of their spiritual path, I also provide a new approach to psychedelics, most easily understood through context. Therefore, before detailing the methodology, I share my personal experiences with psychedelics to provide necessary context. Later in the book, I introduce the method and how it can be applied to your life, not just psychedelic trips.

In the Appendix I include scientific studies and

other need-to-know information on the substances that I used. Many readers have reported that reading the Appendix and then rereading the trips provides ever greater enjoyment and understanding of the psychedelic effect.

Before I go further, I need to state that the decision to write this book did not come without much consideration. Although my inner feeling strongly indicated that this book needed to be written, I was concerned—no, highly concerned that the information presented here could inspire some reckless individuals, who neglect common safety protocols, to harm themselves. While the plants that I discuss in this work all have extremely safe profiles, they need to be respected and treated with care, for not every form of death is physical.

After much consideration I realized that people who read and study before taking psychedelics are also likely to be more respectful of psychedelics, and therefore more likely to explore them safely. Please prove me right.

My hope is that this work be of some aid to you in your life and on your path of awakening, regardless of whether you incorporate psychedelics into your path. It is not my intent to persuade the reader one way or the other, regarding psychedelics, but instead, to offer a fresh perspective that will help you to have penetrating clarity in all that you do.

Many readers are doubtlessly more experienced with psychedelics than I am, so I am not writing this work as an expert on hallucinogens. Honestly, human beings know so little about these substances that it might be arrogant for anyone to claim expertise on this topic. Instead, what I am offering is an approach to life that also applies extremely well to psychedelic journeys.

Surely there are many readers who have yet to try psychedelics but who feel drawn to do so at some point along their paths. It is my hope that the approach, information, and resources provided here will help those individuals to have greater understanding of and respect for psychedelics before jumping in.

To those individuals who are convinced that psychedelics have no place on the path of awakening, I know exactly how you feel, for I too held that view for the majority of my own process. Even if you find yourself opposed to the use of psychedelics, it is my hope that you find my approach to life useful and stimulating.

In my case, were it not for an unexpected, deep inner pull that led me to the Amazon, I might never have questioned my ideology. Even with the strong inner knowing that I should take ayahuasca, I did not enter the world of psychedelics lightly, and, in my opinion, neither should anyone else. Whatever the individual chooses on the path of awakening is ultimately the responsibility of the individual—or at least it is wise to behave as if that were the case.

In this work I often describe a "pulling feeling." The pull is a powerful sign of inner guidance that should not be confused with a common compulsion or urge. It is of a different nature entirely. The more that one follows this pull, when it arises, the more powerful its guidance becomes in your life.

In a way, following the pull requires a leap of faith, for often it will lead you to face your fears and do things that you have been avoiding, despite knowing deep down that those things are right. Sometimes, as is often the case with me, the pull may force you to directly confront your ideologies and beliefs. Eventually it can become so powerful that your body will begin to move entirely on its own through complex activities, so long as you allow it.

In my estimation, the single most powerful thing that people could do on their paths of awakening is to awaken to the pull, for that is your guidance system on your path. From this place of inner guidance I entered my psychedelic journeys.

If the reader has never experienced such a pull, this book might be easily misunderstood. As there is no way to give the pulling experience to the reader, I must accept that limitation and work around it as best as possible. Just know that the rational mind is but one of the most recently developed areas of the brain. Many other powerful structures in the brain can also serve to guide our lives. I merely ask that you suspend your disbelief while reading, so that you may receive as purely as possible.

Here's to your path of awakening, whatever it may entail!

CHAPTER 1

the vine of souls

In late June of 2009, I joined an ecotour group in Ecuador. We spent several days traveling around the country by bus, going from the capital city of Quito to the cloud forest of the Andes, then into the lowland jungles to the headwaters of the Amazon River. We flew into the jungle via a prop-driven Cessna plane, piloted by an Achuar tribesman. Once we landed, we canoed to a small village that had been constructed by the Achuar specifically for ecotourism. We spent a few days at this camp, where we lived in Achuar-made, palm leaf-covered huts, and we hiked through the surrounding jungle to learn about the local flora and fauna.

After a few days we were invited by a shaman in a nearby village to take part in a traditional natem ceremony. *Natem* is the local word for a powerful psychedelic commonly known as ayahuasca, "the vine of the soul." We were given detailed information on what to expect once we arrived at the village, what the ceremony would entail, and how to safely navigate the ayahuasca experience. We were all eager to begin our three-hour hike to that village the next day. Those of us who were intending to receive the ayahuasca began fasting.

We left the next afternoon for a silent, prayerful hike to the shaman's village, led by our Achuar guide. I think I was still a bit nervous at the idea of taking ayahuasca. I didn't have a very positive view of mind-altering substances because, as a young man, I had used marijuana and alcohol to escape. A lot of resultant suffering followed my misguided use of those substances. Although we had been told that ayahuasca would not alter our sense of self, I was still somewhat suspicious, even as I felt strongly drawn to take it.

A few hours into our trek, we came across some fresh jaguar tracks. The Achuar guide indicated that the cat had passed only minutes earlier, and that our presence had probably scared it off. The tracks, each of them larger than my palm, were clearly visible on the trail. We were in the thick of it, for sure! Unexpectedly, the inspiration I felt from seeing those paw prints put me at ease about the upcoming ceremony.

As we neared the village, we took time to spread out and find solo sit-spots where we could privately construct a list of questions to be answered through the ceremony. After assembling my list, I had a strong feeling that the ayahuasca vision would provide guidance for my life's mission.

We remained in our sit-spots for 30 minutes before we continued our trek. Within a few minutes we came to a deep, flowing creek with a large fallen tree bridging its banks. A loinclothed Achuar villager looked on in amusement as our guide led us across the creek. We continued through a small valley and up a hill to a clearing atop it that overlooked a vast Amazon tributary. There at the flat center of the hill were two large community huts. We had arrived.

It was already well into afternoon at the time, so we set up our tents near the manioc gardens, a bit away from the main tribal huts.

After setting up our tents, we gathered to discuss the upcoming ceremony and to decide who was going to take the natem and who was planning to help. The helpers assist journeyers in getting to a secure place in the forest for some privacy and safety, and they lead the journeyer back safely once the visionary experience is complete.

We waited in silence near the edge of a high cliff for the sun to set over the vast tributary that flowed below us. The ceremony was soon to begin. About a half hour later, when it was dark enough, we were led to the shaman's hut and asked to sit on benches around the pillared, open-air rim of the space.

The shaman was an elderly gentleman in traditional attire with an orange, parrot-feathered headband. He was clearly in deep prayer as he stirred the cauldron of neon-orange natem. He whispered in a songlike rhythm as he blew tobacco smoke into the brew, which had been simmering for most of the day. He stirred the natem with clear affection, and then he turned and greeted us.

The ceremony began as he directed me to sit on a stool in front of him. He blessed me with a feather and then gazed at me before he filled a large, decorated clay bowl to the brim with natem. Through a translator, I was told to drink all the liquid quickly. After downing the bitter stuff, I was given some water to wash out my mouth.

Although we were told that the effects of natem would probably start about an hour after consumption, I was feeling something strange within 15 minutes. My entire vascular system began to vibrate, and my blood felt electric. Because we were told that ayahuasca comes on slowly, I thought I might be imagining the strange feelings. Within a minute, dizziness overtook me, and I told my helper, Larry.

"You're imagining things," Larry said. "Fifteen minutes is way too quick for effects to begin." I told him that I was about to puke, and without delay, he guided me away from the hut to the edge of the forest.

My eyes must have been dilated, because the light from the shaman's hut was overwhelming. I lost all sense of direction and was unable to stand on my own. It was the most disorienting experience of my life.

Larry kindly took my arm over his shoulder and guided me safely to our destination. Once there, I got on my hands and knees to purge before I rolled onto my back, thankful to the earth for holding me steady. A mosquito landed on my forehead and speared my third eye. I felt a pinch, and with that I closed my eyes—the journey had begun.

I heard an undulating vibration like that of millions of cicada in chorus. As the sound intensified, I could feel an energetic pressure rising from the base of my body up to the top of my head, threatening to blow like a volcano. By the time the energy reached the crown of my skull, it was a screaming, high-pitched, frenzy of intensity that finally exploded from the top of my head.

I found myself sitting, eyes open, on the jungle floor during the day. A small, light-blue butterfly fluttered just before me. It had a dot on each wing that looked like eyes. The butterfly fluttered off just as the image of a boldly colored fluorescent lizard flashed before me. Then I found my perspective no longer in the forest but instead in the heart of the earth. A frighteningly powerful voice addressed me. My lesson had begun.

The voice started by teaching me the purpose of life on Earth. I was shown rapidly approaching societal destruction and the renewal to follow. I was taught of the coming of Christ and the resulting shift that would cascade throughout humanity. I was shown that humanity is on the verge of an incredible enlightenment that would come with the mass exposure of corruption rampant at all levels of society. I saw that the three pillars of humanity—economy, ecology, and society—will soon fail.

I was shown that consciousness from the center of the galaxy will be bathing the solar system with ever-increasing intensity. And with this intensity, the corruption, greed, and selfishness that run through society will cause civilization to implode, destroying everything around it.

I was shown that the attitude people take toward the changes in society will determine one of two possible futures. If people selfishly resist positive change, the human population, as well as most of the flora and fauna of the planet, will be reduced to near-extinction levels.

Suddenly, I found myself immersed in the unbearable suffering of humanity. Although there were no images, what I felt is well beyond my capacity to describe.

Then I was removed from that hell and shown the second possibility. If humans choose to embrace the changes with a positive attitude, determined to learn and to live in a way that loves and honors all of life, then things won't be quite as difficult.

I was dipped into the hellish suffering represented by this possible future. Even in this lesser hell, the mass suffering was beyond my comprehension. Due to the momentum of our societal structures, I was shown that mass suffering was unavoidable. The only question remaining was the degree of suffering that we would experience on this planet. I so wanted to know whether there was some other path that didn't result in hell, but ayahuasca denied me.

After the collapse, I saw that the remaining population would transition into a truly inspiring, enlightened way of life. People will live positive, inspired lives in communion with all things. I was shown that, after the collapse, what we now call miracles will be considered perfectly normal and natural.

I saw how truly important attitude is to the awakening process. It is wise to treat our experience on Earth as we might a school and a teacher. Use the experiences that life offers as opportunities to exercise a positive, loving attitude. The experiences will not always be pleasant, and many will be hard. But consider any good sports coach. Does that coach baby us in hopes that we will gain skill and ability? Not at all. The coach challenges us to our limits, and sometimes even beyond, knowing that through hard training we will gain ability and strength. How well we do is dependent upon how coachable we are. Consider that the Earth experience is training, but instead of adding through this training, we are stripping away all that is blocking us from our deepest, innermost harmony.

I saw an image of the planet wrapped by a serpent that was eating its own tail—the ouroboros. I saw in this symbol the idea that experience is earned by the individual, and that there are no accidents. The head of the snake, representing the present moment, is consuming its own tail, the past.

I was shown that we have created the world we live in through past incarnations, just as we are now creating the world we will be born into in future incarnations.

We get experiences that will challenge us. The attitude that we take toward those experiences is totally up to us. Eventually, when the shallow life that prioritizes pleasure, power, safety, comfort, approval, and distraction fails to satisfy, we will wake up to the training opportunity. Upon taking up the training, we will find the opportunity to realize our fundamental nature, which is harmonious.

I was shown that there are many more people on the planet now who are ready to graduate the school of the Earth than there have ever have been at any time in the history of this planet. First, one person will graduate and light the way for a great enlightenment on Earth.

I was shown that, for roughly the next thousand years, this planet will remain at a high state of harmony and provide a wonderful opportunity to graduate for many individuals. Imagine living in a world where everyone lives positive, inspired lives and seeks understanding, a world where awakening is possible for all. What a beautiful world it would be.

I saw that attitude is the key to awakening, and that an awakened individual has mastered right attitude. We must not seek a savior. Each individual needs to take responsibility for their own path, with integrity, ever opening to the deepest place of being within.

You may have many teachers and guides during your life, but learn from them wisely, without relying on them or trusting them blindly. Do not worship them, for no one is any more or less spiritual than you are.

With right attitude, one learns constantly from others while questioning and testing everything within one's own life. Most importantly, we will begin to learn from our innermost being, through the process of awakening; we will no longer treat the people, the flora, and the fauna of the world merely as resources to be exploited, for we will see the intrinsic value and beauty that is inherent to everything. That doesn't mean we will no longer participate in the harvest. Instead, we will see that harvesting with right attitude is vitally important to maintaining a healthy ecosystem.

I was given instructions to prepare for my mission on Earth. By combining the martial, meditation, and healing arts that I was studying in Japan, I would discover a principle that would then transform those arts into a path of enlightenment that would, in turn, aid many to graduate the school of the earth.

After the vision was over, Larry led me back to the shaman's hut. I was directed to the shaman's table, where I was energetically cleansed with a feather and the shaman's breath. I spent the next few hours lying on the ground, stargazing until my body had normalized enough to walk, and then I returned to my tent and slept for the rest of the night.

I woke up the next morning feeling physically healthy aside from the miserable pain of hemorrhoids that had blown up to the size of a golf ball from the internal pressure generated by the experiences of Hell.

Psychologically, I was in a state of shock, for I could not forget what I was shown of the horrors to come. I wanted to discount the vision, but the more I thought about it, the more I was convinced that our society was sprinting off a cliff. I knew that nations worldwide were suffering social decay, and that the financial system was already careening. After all, it was 2009, just a year after the global financial system almost collapsed. Thanks to corruption in banking and in government, I didn't believe that the banking system was being honestly reformed. And regarding the environment, I could clearly see decline in my own lifetime. Rationally speaking, I could see that all three pillars of civilization were in rapid decline. To me, there simply was no logical escape route for humanity, and that was a depressing realization.

Although we returned to our village later that morning by canoe, I do not remember much of the trip, so immersed within myself was I. I was trying to get a grip on the enormity of what I was shown, but my psychological grasp was just too small for the task. In retrospect, I am sure I was suffering from post-traumatic stress disorder. My own mission regarding the coming changes was too much to digest, so for the rest of the trip, I was pulled into myself and out of touch.

Before the vision I was a highly engaged, positive, leading element in our group, but after the vision, it was as if a switch were flipped. I was quiet and disengaged. Many group members kindly showed concern and tried to get me to speak of my vision, but I felt that sharing the vision was inappropriate, so I remained bottled up for the remainder of the trip.

Several years passed before I had digested enough of the vision to share details with anyone other than my wife and my martial arts instructor. My instructor found the idea of combining the healing, meditation, and martial arts intriguing, so we began training privately for many hours every day—he taught me martial arts, and I taught him meditation and Sotai-ho, a healing art that I was licensed to teach.

As I was living in Japan for the purpose of training, I used the next few years to explore the power of attitude within my training. I was interested in how the unconditioned power of appreciation and love could be applied to the therapy, meditation, and martial arts that I was studying. I was searching for a way of being that expedited the path of awakening, while simultaneously advancing my studies in the arts.

My martial arts instructor fully supported my search, and by means of inner correction, we progressed rapidly in the arts. After a few years, I received master's licenses in four samurai arts to go along with my license in Sotai-ho. I returned to America to fulfill my responsibilities.

CHAPTER 2

call of the mushroom

The better part of a decade passed before I was drawn
to another psychedelic experience. Inspired by the
curiosity of one of my students regarding psilocybin
mushrooms, I acquired 7.5 grams, a "heroic dose," of
the fungi for my exploration into the realm of the
entheogen.

I placed the dried mushrooms in the freezer to
maintain their potency. About a month went by
without a pull to take the mushrooms. Each day, I
wondered whether I would feel the call to take them—
but time and again, nothing.

Late on an unusually warm winter afternoon I felt a pull, but it wasn't toward the freezer. Instead, my body headed out the front door and into the forest, toward some unknown destination. The body moved with urgency and purpose. It hopped the fence of my property and headed up a winding trail into the mountains, dodging the rough buckbrush branches as it followed a deer trail-tunnel through the thick foliage that finally opened into a small meadow.

In the center was a mound of dirt like a small hill that had a vague ring around it, about five feet in diameter, the track of an ancient ponderosa pine that once stood hundreds of feet over the area. This mound was the only proof that it ever existed. Digging down into the dirt at the top of the mound I found the warm pithy wood still decomposing.

My body moved counterclockwise around the base of the mound, scuffing the ground with my shoes to draw a clear circle around the tree's former position. After the circle was delineated, my hands began clearing away all debris. My breathing quickened from the inspiration and purpose rushing through my body, the vibration intensifying so that it felt as if my body was going to explode spontaneously from the top of my head, becoming an eternal partner with the torrential spirit of that long-gone tree.

After all debris was removed, my body sat facing the center, cross-legged on the ground, spine erect, with my back just inside the edge of the circle. I wondered why my body was drawn to this spot and what I was to be taught.

My mind filled with myriad images of birth and

death, from the birth and death of the universe itself, to galaxies, solar systems, all the way down to the conception of life, cell division, childbirth, aging, and finally death before repeating again.

My mind was exploring the grand cycle of birth and death. I could see that this process was related to the death of my cousin, Ethan, who had passed just a few days earlier on his 11th birthday. For days I had felt his presence around me, singing and dancing. Ethan was an extraordinary child, a living fountain of love and joy. His death was so unexpected. It was from such a sensitive place that this visionary process began.

I sat perfectly still, observing the grand images of the birth and death cycle for about a half hour, judging by the setting sun, before my body rose to step out of the circle. The visionary process was finished with me for now, so I headed back to the warmth of my house.

I explained to my wife about the visionary experience that I had just gone through and that I would need to spend some quiet time later in the evening in prolonged meditation. At that moment, I knew I was to take the mushrooms, the pull undeniable.

My wife was preparing a lovely steak dinner. I knew that eating anything before consuming psilocybin mushrooms would probably cause nausea, yet despite this knowledge, there was a powerful knowing that, for my experience, I was to eat the full meal and then take the mushrooms. I suspected that I was in for quite a journey.

I enjoyed a full meal, then I prepared a mushroom brew by simmering the 7.5 grams in a pot of water for 20 minutes, while in deep prayer. Although I was preparing the brew in front of my wife, I intentionally omitted telling her anything about the nature of these mushrooms. As I commonly made my own home-brew herbal concoctions, she thought nothing of my activities. Technically, I didn't hide my consumption, but, in my heart of hearts, I was avoiding this issue, for I did not wish to argue with her about taking psychedelics.

Although she had never explicitly spoken against the use of psychedelics, I suspected that she would be opposed to the idea. I didn't want to have an argument before taking mushrooms, for to evoke negative emotions before a psychedelic trip can cause a lot of suffering once in the full grip of the experience.

I quickly drank the liquid and ate the remaining mushrooms at the bottom of the glass, and then I headed back to the bedroom for privacy. Once seated in the bedroom, I took a moment to pray: "What is death? What am I not understanding about life? And what is still veiling my consciousness? Show me my remaining darkness."

The memory of Ethan came up again, and I wondered what could be learned from his death. I heard his voice in the back of my mind, "Be happy—no excuses. Tell the family to be happy, with no excuses. Tell everyone to be happy!"

I thought I was happy ...

CHAPTER 3

naked and afraid

Within minutes of sitting, I found myself in a deep, powerful silence. Energy seemed to course through my body, buoying it. It was a great feeling to start my first psilocybin trip, I thought. The buoying feeling didn't last long, however. Within just a few minutes, the experience took an uncomfortable turn. I began feeling a bit sick to my stomach. I assumed it wasn't serious, so, at first, I ignored it, attempting to go further into silence.

The nausea rapidly escalated, so I dove deeper into meditation, hoping it would relieve my stomach. Before long, I was forced to choose between throwing up in my bedroom and rushing to the bathroom. I rose from my seated position on wobbly legs and staggered into the bathroom for release, purposely neglecting to tell my wife of my precarious situation.

I positioned myself at the toilet for a time, but nothing came up. After waiting for a few minutes, the pressure in my stomach began to subside, as I felt a gurgle in my bowels. I realized that the tea had taken a turn south, so I quickly repositioned myself for a different explosion. Although I had the feeling that I was about to blow, and the extreme discomfort that entails, the release didn't come.

While sitting on the toilet, a chill came over my body, which began shivering. Taking the risk of blowing out all over the floor, I rose to turn on the bath water, in hopes of warming myself. About the time the bath filled halfway, the chills turned to profuse sweating as my body temperature soared.

It was a cold winter evening, and the bathroom temperature was about 50 degrees Fahrenheit, but at that moment it felt more like 120 degrees. I hurriedly stripped off all my clothing, turned off the bath water, and laid myself down on the cold ceramic floor to cool down. It felt so good—for a moment.

In an instant, my body took another turn to trembling cold, and to make things worse, I had to pee like never before, so I staggered back to the toilet and took wobbly aim. My body was so cold that I couldn't relax enough to release. It was as if someone had locked it and tossed away the key. It hurt badly.

It then occurred to me that maybe someone had made a mistake and accidentally mixed some poisonous mushrooms in with the hallucinogenic types. After all, little brown galerina mushrooms, which are some of the deadliest mushrooms known, commonly grow right next to psilocybin mushrooms. I began to panic.

Fortunately, I'd carried a pen and some note paper into the bathroom with me in the event that I needed to write something important. With shaking hand, I managed to fumble my way through "I think I ate poisonous mushrooms, please tell this to the doctor!" I set the paper down and decided to wait a bit longer before calling out to my wife. I didn't want to take a trip to the emergency room for no reason, after all.

Suddenly all three exits warned of release, so I abandoned the pen and plopped myself back onto the toilet seat. I picked up the little trash can that sits next to the bowl and placed it on my lap to throw up into. There I was, a grown man, naked, shivering, and literally begging for a triple explosion, with my head buried in a wastebasket. My entire nervous system was so hyped up that my skin hurt to touch anything, even lightly. My breathing was labored, my pulse was racing, and my head throbbed unbearably.

I had a sudden third-person image of myself looking like a sagging question mark, and I realized how ridiculous I appeared in that moment. I thought, "I'm in really bad shape. Maybe I should call out for help ... no ... I don't want to bother her. I'll pull through as soon as I purge. I just need to get this out."

Suddenly my temperature rose again, and my pores covered my body in slippery sweat. In panic, I called out to my wife before I swooned off the toilet onto the cold tile floor, half-conscious.

As soon as I hit the floor, my mind began spinning, faster and faster, as if I were trapped in some insane amusement park ride. I closed my eyes hoping to center myself, but that only made things much, much worse.

Try as I might, my eyes refused to open again. My stomach, bowels, and bladder all ached for release, but I no longer had any control over my body. I realized that I was about to release on the floor and ... on myself.

Desperately, I attempted to call out to my wife, but my mouth refused to follow my intention. My tongue felt like a dry twig in my mouth, a sign of severe dehydration. I couldn't move, felt dehydrated, and was at risk of hypothermia, too, if I didn't warm up soon. The knowledge I had from the survival courses I had taken told me that death was a real possibility in this situation. An image flashed in my mind's eye of my dead body, naked on the cold tile floor, my partner just outside, none the wiser. Somehow I had the impression that I had been tricked into this precarious situation.

CHAPTER 4

the trickster

I faded into a dreamlike visionary state in which an evil tricksterish demon's cackling laughter jarred my nerves. "Finally, I have you! I've been waiting a long time for this moment. Now you are mine, and there is no escape. You should have called out to your wife while you had the chance, but you didn't want to be a bother. You are about to die, and you won't call to your wife for fear of annoying her. Ha! That's not love! Now you'll lie here unattended until you suffer brain damage, or your body dies, or both. She doesn't really love you. No one does. How does it feel knowing that you may die alone in your own excrement?"

I realized that I had spent my entire life avoiding reliance on others and seeking total independence. Although I was happy to help others in need, I could not ask help for myself. Was it pride, arrogance, insecurity? Whatever it was, it was clear that this demon was going to put my nose in it, while I soiled myself. "God, I hope I don't soil myself," I thought.

The trickster said, "You're so screwed up! You care more about your wife having to clean up the mess of your death than you do about actually dying. That's not love. You've never been loved, and now you know that your marriage is false. Oh, you love her, but you feel deep down that she doesn't love you. What is your marriage based on? Convenience?"

I realized that the real issue in my marriage was that I didn't want to bother my wife by asking her for help. I didn't want to bother anyone. I didn't consider myself to be worth the bother. I didn't consider myself worthy of others' time and energy. This demon was clever. He seemed to smell psychological disharmony like a shark senses blood in the water, and he knew exactly where to sink his teeth.

His power was such that my mind was entirely trapped, and I could do nothing to resist him. I couldn't open my eyes or move my body. My teeth chattered, and my body shivered violently as my temperature rapidly dropped. All I had to do to warm up was get in the water or flip on the overhead heat lamp, but I had no authority over my body or my mind.

I vowed that even if I died, I would use this experience to purify my soul. I realized that I could use this demon's talent for detecting my weaknesses to my advantage, even if it killed my body. I would use this demon like a disharmony detector, to release and resolve whatever he force-fed me. I had no ability to stop him, so I was determined to make the best of the situation by facing my fears and insecurities.

With that awareness, suddenly, I was free. I awoke on the floor, naked and cold, my fever gone. I still had stomach, bowel, and bladder releasing to do, so I got back on the toilet and resumed my question mark pose. I called out to my wife in a strong, clear voice asking her to come into the bathroom. I had to face my insecurity.

"Are you okay?" she said from the other side of the door.

"No, I am feeling pretty sick. I think I may have diarrhea, and I have to vomit. I think they both might come at the same time. Can you get me a bucket? I don't want to use this trash can if I don't have to. I had chills and a fever, but they seem to have gone now. I need you to stay with me for a bit to make sure I don't fall off the toilet and knock myself out. I should tell you that I ate a lot of hallucinogenic mushrooms, and they seem to disagree with me. If you end up having to take me to the emergency room, please tell the doctor about the mushrooms."

"You are so stupid. You should have told me. Let me get you a bucket. I'll be right back." She returned quickly with the bucket. I put my head into the bucket while I sat on the toilet. I saw another image of myself looking like a human roly-poly, balled up into myself.

"I'm so grateful that you're here to help me," I said.

She sat there, on the edge of the bathtub, and watched me nervously. I asked her to keep talking. Focusing on her voice helped me to stabilize my mind. I was fearful that I might drop back into the nightmarelike state if I lost concentration. I could feel it just at the edge of my consciousness.

"What shall I talk about?"

"Anything .... Tell me what's on your mind."

She began talking about Ethan, my second cousin who had died just a few days earlier. Ethan had a grand mal seizure that rendered him instantly brain-dead. His body was kept alive by machines for days, but there was no detectable brain activity, so his parents ultimately had to let him go.

"I'm so worried about the family. I can't even imagine what Ethan's mother must be feeling now. No mother should have to bury her child. It's awful. I wonder if there's anything we can do to help the family get through this hardship?"

"Yes, me too," I said. "It seems to me that when someone dies, it's the people left behind that really suffer .... I'm sorry to change the topic, but I am getting too weak and dizzy to keep my balance on this toilet. I think I am going to have to lie down, but I'm afraid that I may end up releasing on the floor."

"It's okay. You're sick. It can't be helped."

"I'm not just sick in a normal sense. This is part of a visionary process that I am going through. I am being shown my hidden and latent disharmony. It's horrible and terrifying, but I need to go through this.

I need to be alone now, but maybe you could check in on me every now and again."

"Of course."

Suddenly I was alone, back in the hellish vision surrounded by the echoing cackles of the demon. "You realize she never came to your aid, right? That was all an illusion in your mind. You're still lying naked on the floor dying. You're mine, and you are going insane! I control your mind and your body. What you experience is completely my will."

To emphasize his point, my bladder began to ache as if it would explode. I tried to pee, but I couldn't release. Then, in an instant, the urge was gone. Nausea returned, causing me to reach for the bucket, but just as I was ready, the nausea was replaced by the explosive pressing of diarrhea.

"You are my puppet. I own you!" The demon laughed.

My eyes darted here and there uncontrollably, and my tongue stuck out, waggling. My head turned left and right, out of my control. Strange, unintelligible, childlike words emerged from my mouth repeatedly. I tried to expand my awareness beyond this hell, but to no avail.

"There is no escaping the darkness that your life is based upon," the demon said. "Your corruption is your leash and my whip."

"This must be the judgment," I thought. Only it was not Jesus judging me but Satan! It seemed that Satan was the perfect judge, because he saw right through the structures of my mind to find my inner corruption, like a wolf sees through the herd to find the sick. He knew exactly where to attack. And when he struck, the result was so overwhelming, so complete, that there was no place to hide, no path of escape, no way to fight back.

Oh, how I wished for the misery to end. But somehow I knew this was just the beginning.

CHAPTER 5

first corruption

The demon chuckled and said, "You do remember, don't you? It was you who prayed to be to be shown your unseen darkness. Be thankful, for your prayer has been answered. I hope you enjoy it. I'm having a marvelous time."

Yes, I had prayed to see my remaining disharmony, but I wasn't expecting *this!*

Time disappeared, and I found myself in the strange, dark recesses of my own twisted mind. I felt utterly insane, my thoughts corrupted and nonsensical. I could hear disturbing, discombobulated gibberish, coming from my mouth. Images and feelings began streaming through— arguments, yelling, spankings, and fights. I felt unseen, unwanted, unsupported, unworthy, and in the way.

The strange utterances brought to my mind the image of a toddler trying to formulate words. I felt an overarching feeling of negativity and deep disagreement with life. I was astonished that a toddler could feel such things.

I realized that my disagreement with life had so impregnated the formation of my words that it ran throughout all of my language, and, therefore, my thought, for language is the basis for human thought.

This corruption was a cornerstone of my personality as I grew. It tainted my self-image, my thinking, my social strategies, relationships, job choices, and everything else to some degree.

I realized that I was seeing my own childhood developmental process. How sad it was to have lived so long with such negativity. It caused so much pain over time, but because it was present in me from such a young age, it had been normalized. It was simply who I was. I knew nothing different, so it went entirely under the radar of my awareness. I was just going through life reacting in accordance with this programming, unable even to question it.

Because I felt unsupported as a child, once I became a young adult, I began spending all of my energy seeking total independence from others, so as to be "out of the way." Through training in the martial arts and survival, my self-reliance grew little by little.

This virtue became pride that was actually rooted in a fundamental sense of unworthiness.

Ethan's voice came to me again: "Be happy—no excuses."

"How? How can I be happy when my very sense of self is born of unhappiness?" I said.

I could see that each person has, as the very basis of the sense of self, some negativity that determines the direction of more sophisticated characteristics. It is like the speck of dust that determines the form of a snowflake.

"Ethan, you're asking the impossible!"

CHAPTER 6

promises amiss

Spasms overtook my body, my head pivoting back and forth, eyes darting here and there, and tongue wagging like a dry twig in the wind.

"I'm so thirsty! So much pain! Unbearable! God, make it stop!" These thoughts wound through my mind before it went white. Time and the world disappeared, leaving only insanity.

Eventually, something shifted, and I found myself in an unknown space. I wasn't sure whether I was dead or alive, or whether I had ever lived at all. "If I'm alive, I must be insane," I thought. "Maybe I am an old man housed in a psychiatric ward, no more than a drooling gork, with occasional glimpses back on times of relative sanity. Or maybe my last moment of sanity was the lovely dinner I had with my wife before disappearing into the bedroom to meditate, the story of my life but a distant memory of my youth. Or maybe my entire life story was the construct of an insane mind. Maybe I'm not the person I thought I was. Maybe Richard never existed at all."

Through the haze of insanity, images of a woman came to the fore. Somehow, I felt that I knew and loved this person dearly, but I wasn't sure whether the memories were real or imaginary. Then I remembered the promise that I made in a vision as a child, to dedicate my life in the search for spiritual truth. "Surely, these are real memories," I thought. "They feel so powerful! If only I could have another chance."

The trickster seized on the opportunity: "Ah, but you won't get another chance. You won't survive this. Your body is dying, and no one will help you. You've wasted your life. What a glorious waste!"

It was then that I remembered that I was in the early stage of publishing my first book, *The Unbound Soul*, which fulfilled part of a promise that I made as a young boy.

My mind flashed back to my childhood promise, a promise that became my life compass and a counterbalance to my inner darkness.

Around age eight I began having a recurring dream of Jesus Christ. Just before the onset of these dreams, I had joined a Bible study class, and as a result I became quite interested in the story of Jesus' life as told by Luke, John, Mark, and Matthew. I was totally captivated by the character of Jesus and found myself thinking of him daily.

Most of what I read about Jesus was beyond my understanding, of course, but for some reason I read every night, unbeknownst even to my own parents. I had a learning disorder, so I never willingly read anything apart from the New Testament.

Our neighborhood Bible study teacher had strongly encouraged us to convert our parents to Christianity. One night, after a failed attempt to convert my parents, my idealistic view of the Bible was shattered. I was set adrift in confusion.

My father had taken the time to walk me through various biblical passages and show me the inconsistencies, which were too obvious for me to ignore. In my innocence I had trusted my Bible study teacher, but I realized that she had led me astray.

I thought about the inconsistencies and cruelty of this unjust God that is portrayed in the Bible. I wondered if our Bible study teacher had lied to us, or if she too was just as misled and confused as I was.

I so badly wanted to know the truth that Jesus spoke of in the Bible, when he said, "Know the truth and the truth will set you free." I wanted to be free, and I felt that there must be some truth to his story. My father honestly admitted that he didn't know the truth as proclaimed by Jesus, and he confided that he didn't think anyone else did either.

Until that moment I thought my father knew everything. I certainly didn't think adults would intentionally mislead me, at least not until I joined Bible study. In the aftermath of my father's admission I was no longer so sure.

The turmoil in my mind lasted for months. I so desperately wanted the truth that Jesus spoke of in the Bible, but I knew no one whom I could trust who was also in a position to know.

My grandparents were Christian, but they told me the very same thing that my Bible study teacher taught, which was that anyone who was not Born Again would go to hell, even if they were Christian.

I tried going to church with them a few times, but I heard the same hellfire and damnation speech that I was getting at Bible study. My trust in adults was faltering.

"Was God so cruel and spiteful," I wondered, "that he would send people to hell forever for not believing in the Bible? Even just for questioning?"

I could not understand how God's punishment, eternal damnation, helped people to better themselves. It just seemed like the worst form of cruelty. I didn't like that God! "Why would Jesus love God, if God were cruel?"

Some weeks after talking with my father, I awoke within a dream-state that felt more real than reality. The room was aglow with a subtle emanation. There on the floor, spread in front of me, was a robed stranger with long, dark hair.

I should have been terrified that a strange man was in my room in the depths of night, but I felt not the slightest hint of fear. I got out of bed and approached the man. Although his head did not move, his eyes tracked me as I approached.

"Are you all right?" I asked as I looked into his eyes. I was captivated by the deep wellsprings that were his eyes. It felt like I was looking into eternal love. Upon locking gazes, I knew. I can't explain how I knew, but I knew—this was Jesus Christ.

In a slow voice he said, "Help me."

I assumed he wanted me to help him up, so I took hold of his left arm, but it warped in my grip like a water balloon. I tried to pull him up, but his body just sagged beneath me. It was then that I realized that he had no skeleton. I stepped back in astonishment. I looked back into his eyes, hoping for an explanation.

"Help me," he repeated.

I awoke sweating, crying, and confused.

This dream repeated again and again over the next several months. The details were always the same, as if I were stuck in a time loop, but while in the dream state, I could never recall the earlier dreams. I always awoke the same way, crying and confused. Only after awakening did I recall the previous dreams. Paradoxically, though I dreaded those dreams, I also yearned for them. I hated the feeling of helplessness, but I wanted to see Jesus again.

One night it ended. The dream began as it always had, but just at the point where Jesus asked for my help the second time, the point where the dream always ended, a surge of energy shot through my body, anchoring me in the dream. Immediately, I asked, "How can I help you?"

"Find my bones, for they represent the core of my teaching. Most of what is written about me is untrue.

41

Mankind has so twisted my teachings for selfish gain that little of the essence remains. What little remains is largely overlooked in the religious ritual and confusion. Find the essence of my teachings and give it back to the world. That is how you can help. Will you do this?"

As a child, I didn't fully understand the ramifications of what I was being asked to do, but I felt a strong sense of rightness, so I gave my solemn oath.

Although that was the last time Jesus visited me in a dream, I had made a promise, and I intended to keep it.

"Such a cruel joke life is," I thought. In my teens, I almost committed suicide because I felt unworthy of my promise to Jesus. Were it not for a spiritual intervention that saved and redirected my life, I would not be suffering. I had always assumed that intervention was a blessing, but I was having second thoughts.

By the time I was 16 years old, I was so self-critical, so down on myself that I no longer wished to live. I was in such a weak state of mind that I was living an entirely fake life, surrounded by friends who were interested only in getting high and drinking.

One summer afternoon I decided that I could no longer stand myself. I could do nothing right, and my mind was constantly comparing me to everyone else, a comparison that I never won. I hated everything that I had ever said, felt, thought, or done. I hated even the faintest hint of me—my very soul. I just wanted it to end.

I sat next to my bed with suicide note in hand and method set. I couldn't understand why Jesus had come to me for help, when I clearly was unable to follow through. I had failed to keep my promise, but I wasn't going to fail at this.

I had heard stories of people slitting their wrists only to live with the scars. Then there were the stories of people who took pills, only to end up in a hospital getting their stomachs pumped. Oh, and the people who put a bullet through their temples only to survive with no frontal lobe. Jumping off a tall building seemed like a sure way to go, but then you have the horror of the fall, and sometimes people survive those falls, living with broken bodies. No, I was going to do this right—a hollow-point bullet through my mouth into the back of my brain.

You know, it's strange how we tend to think of suicidal people as being irrational. For my part, I was very rational. I could see no possibility for improvement, only continued suffering, while consuming more resources. In such a circumstance, suicide seemed the most logical action, the only escape.

Knowing that my last moment was upon me, I relaxed deeply in the realization that I no longer had a future to fear or past to regret. I no longer needed to pretend to be someone else. I no longer had to suffer from the endless inner-critic. I no longer needed to *be*—a wonderful thought. I released myself.

Thought ceased ...

I was in a deeply relaxed, clear silence for a time, before my eyes were drawn upward to see the rays of afternoon light pouring into the room. The rays intersected with particles of dust in the air to cause a sparkling light show. The little sparkles appeared to be tiny angels of light dancing in the air. It was one of the most inspiring moments of my life. Then something happened that was unimaginable. Energy surged through my body, and a voice rang forth from my chest, which vibrated like a bell. I don't know if anyone else could have heard this voice, but it was clear, loving, and directive:

"You can change your life. You can stop spending time with those who are selfish and negative, who don't really care about you. You can stop drinking and smoking. You can find friends who are working for something positive, who have a purpose in life that you respect. You can go to college, even if only part-time. Make your life full of positive purpose. You are free to do what you feel is right. Do what you want to do, and be yourself."

It honestly felt as if an angel had spoken through my body. Had it been my own voice or that of another person, no matter how much I had respected them, I would not have believed I could do what was suggested. But for some reason that I can't sufficiently explain, I knew that I could accomplish what I set out to do.

My life changed dramatically in an instant. In short order I had weaned myself of negatively directed people, and I began seeking my own path.

Since that time, I've devoted my entire life to

fulfilling my childhood promise. For 30 years, I have researched martial, meditation, and healing arts, traveling the world and seeking the truth as I had promised, with the intent to share what I found with the world.

Finally, I had something worth sharing in the form of an unpublished manuscript, and here I was about to die before seeing it through.

The trickster chimed in: "Your message is lost. No one will ever read it. You've failed your promise. Your life is an absolute failure. I've waited your whole life to witness this moment. Now I've got you, and I'll never let you go."

I was aware of my body again. It was so cold now. My body ached for water. Apparently, I wasn't dead. I tried to call out to my wife, but before I could, my brain was flooded with such intense waves of insanity that it seemed to be cooking. My eyes darted back and forth as my dry tongue stuck out like a white flag from a foxhole. I could hear the babbling again.

Years seemed to pass ...

CHAPTER 7

the fundament

Finally things shifted and images of my early childhood flashed before me. The strange babbling continued, sounds laden heavily with disdain for life.

To my friends and family, there may have been no obvious indication that I was suffering from such underlying feelings, for even I had been previously unaware of this underlying negativity. In fact, I had long thought of myself as a positive person.

Although my conscious perception seemed to be positive, its actual foundation was to some degree born of disagreement with life. My positive thinking was just a way of covering over these feelings like icing on a crapcake. The negativity was subtle and at such a fundamental level that I was largely unaware of it, even long past my day of attempted suicide.

Sure, my childhood was rough, but I'd thought I had gone past those things years earlier. I was mistaken. The negativity was right there all along, hidden in my language, the very foundation of thought and expression, a pillar of the sense of self.

With this realization, I was free of the suffering. The demonic trickster transformed into an angelic being before me. The angel addressed me, saying, "In your life you have made two promises, one to Jesus and one to your wife. Both of these promises are vital, and you have dedicated your entire life to them. This is good, but there is a correction necessary for you to fulfill either of these promises, if that is your true wish."

"Yes, that is and always has been my deepest wish," I replied.

In a booming voice the angel yelled, "The arrogance! The audacity! You wrote a book intending to divulge the truth. To think that anyone can pass along these things—it's utter audacity! Even I cannot explain truth!"

Confused, I asked, "Isn't my book in keeping with my promise to Jesus? Aren't I supposed to publish it? Is the book wrong?"

"It's not that it is wrong. It is as 'correct' as a book ever could be, and it will help a great many people, but do not assume that the inner mystery can ever be taught or even understood. It is arrogance to think

47

that the great mystery could be understood. This is where you have gone amiss. You can only guide people towards the experience of the great mystery. You cannot explain it."

The angel paused in silent repose before continuing in a soft voice: "Each person must experience and explore the inner mystery through their own process. The experience of Oneness is found through grace, in the awareness of silence, and by seeing through the disharmony that has been veiling perception, much like you have this evening.

"Your book will inspire many to the search, so in this regard, it is right to publish, but it is arrogant to think that a book can reveal the essential truth, for each individual will hear your words through their biases, assumptions, and misunderstandings. Their inner demons will twist it this way and that. There is no getting around this fact of life. They must do the work themselves by committing to the exploration. You can't do it for them."

Again, the angel paused for emphasis before continuing. "The sacred limitation is not an accident, nor is it a mistake. Accept the limitation and clean up any such assumptions in your book before publishing."

"Thank you for clarifying this point. My other promise was to my wife. Is there anything that I need to correct in my understanding of our relationship?"

"Be aware that even when she resists or argues with you, the struggle comes from love, even if she is unaware of that love in that moment. Even disharmony is born of love, but you have yet to fully see the connection. There is no other, only Oneness, so even the most heinous disharmony imaginable ultimately stems from that Oneness, even if all involved have no conscious awareness of the connection."

"I don't see it," I said. "Where is the connection to love when someone is killed in a hate-crime? How can that have any connection to love?"

"As the pure energy of love is filtered through a mind structured around misunderstanding, that energy gets distorted into a dark form, becoming a veil that further blocks the perception of Oneness—of love. As this distortion runs through the sense of self, feelings and thoughts grow darker and darker. As these feelings and thoughts are rooted in the self, which ultimately is the sense of separation, one's sense of self becomes increasingly disharmonious through unconscious reactions to the natural feedback loop of life.

"One of the principles of consciousness is that which is within is shared with the world either directly or indirectly, overtly or subtly. Thus, the disharmony that we feel within naturally reflects into the world. Once in the world, the disharmony is then reflected back at the individual. But whether we realize it or not, love is still at the very core of all that we experience; it is merely distorted by misunderstanding, and the individual's fight, flight, freeze reaction to the moment.

"The frustration, loneliness and lost feeling that you felt as a child became a foundational structure of self, which then obscured the perception of love. The feelings of connectedness and unconditioned love were effectively inaccessible to you, even though these things are always present in actuality.

"For you, the fundamental distortion was a disagreement with life itself, and upon this fundamental disagreement, all other life strategies were formulated. The same principle is true for the murderer, the thief, and for anyone who perceives life solely through the mind, which includes almost everyone.

"At a deep level, people judge experiences based upon their desire for love even if they are unaware of this desire or the judgment. When people's experiences come up short, they judge them, and with each judgment, more energy is bound into the veil of darkness, the self.

"The process of distortion happens so quickly and thoroughly that people can entirely lose touch with the direct awareness of love in an instant. Although they may be left with a concept of love and an unconscious longing for it, in experience, they are out of touch with it.

"Because of bound-up darkness, individuals spend their entire lives trying to numb themselves from the psychic pain that comes of that darkness through all manner of distraction—hard work, TV, studying, food, chatting, you name it. Any activity, even 'spiritual pursuits,' can become numbing agents when a negative attitude is at the reins of life. This describes most individuals in society, even those who are considered to be healthy and productive.

"Individuals who suffer from more extreme cases

of bound energy develop highly addictive personalities and then drown themselves in their addictions. It could be drugs, sex, gambling, food, games. It could be anything really. Many individuals are unaware that they are punishing themselves through the addiction, but make no mistake: masochism is at the helm, even if unconsciously.

"For some individuals, the longing for love is so painful that they eventually throw even the longing away, becoming sociopathic. They become so existentially nihilistic and resentful that they may wish to destroy themselves, others, and existence itself.

"In your case, instead of taking your frustrations out on others, you directed that energy inwardly. You judged yourself as being unworthy of love. Although you have resolved much of this energy in your life, there was still a taint running through the structures of your mind, as is represented by language, which has tarnished your experience of life to some degree.

"As you had normalized this darkness at a very early age, and lived with it unconsciously since that time, it was hard for you to notice in daily life. For this reason, tonight, your disharmony was greatly amplified, so that you could see it and feel it clearly, undeniably. You have seen it, and now it is for you to explore in your daily life. When the foundational disharmony is resolved, then there is freedom."

CHAPTER 8

full circle

Finally I was released from the vision. I opened my eyes to find myself in full control of my body again, which was filled with a deep, warming love. I was still naked on the floor in the bathroom, but now I was wrapped from head to toe in wool blankets. My wife was there next to me with a thermos of warm water and a straw through which to drink. Her face was so beautifully comforting. I realized that she had taken good care of me during my trip to hell, and, for that, I was utterly brimming with gratitude. I had never felt so loved and supported by anyone in my life.

I was so weak that I was unable to raise my own head, so my wife helped me to sit up and drink. The warm water felt wonderful in my parched mouth. I asked my wife how long she had been there with me. She looked surprised and said, "Don't you remember? You called to me about a half-hour after you went into the bedroom to meditate. I came in and you were naked on the toilet, with fever."

"Oh, I had completely forgotten about that. I didn't want to tell you about the mushrooms, but my body made me do it—I really had no choice. My body temperature normalized, then it got up, went to the door, opened it, and called out to you, and then you came ... but later, I thought it was an illusion. I didn't think you were really in here with me. Did I tell you anything at that time?"

"Yes, you told me that you were feeling very sick because you had ingested mushrooms. You were worried that maybe you had poisoned yourself.

"Yes, that's right! I made a psychedelic mushroom tea just before dinner. I knew that eating dinner was a bad idea, but then a feeling deep inside said that, for my experience, I should eat dinner. I knew that it would probably make me throw up, but the feeling of rightness was so strong, so I ate dinner knowing that I would suffer for it. I didn't say anything about it to you because I thought that you would not like the idea. It felt deeply right to take the mushrooms, but I didn't think you would understand."

"You should have told me!"

"Yes, I can see that now," I said. "I prayed to be shown my unseen darkness, and shortly thereafter I started feeling sick. I went into the bathroom, and then I started feeling extremely guilty for not telling you about drinking the tea. I remember desperately writing on a piece of paper that I drank psychedelic mushroom tea and that I might have poisoned myself. I wanted you to show the message to a doctor in case you had to take me to the hospital. Then the sickness got worse, much worse. I fell down but I couldn't call out to you. I thought I was going to die!

"I remember talking to a demon that was punishing me. Through his attacks, I discovered the real reason I didn't want to call out to you. I didn't want to bother you. It was a love issue. I have spent my entire life not wanting to bother anyone. I unconsciously felt unworthy of love and support. That's when my body got up and called out to you. I'm so thankful for that! It may seem hard to believe, but I really didn't have a choice in the matter—I had to tell you. It was not negotiable. My body literally did it against my will."

"Yes, you said that you were feeling sick, and that you wanted me to talk to you so you could maintain focus. You were worried that you might pass out. You told me about your love issue, and then we talked about your recently passed cousin and the family. You explained that you were learning about your unresolved disharmony, and that this terrible process was necessary, and that I shouldn't worry. Then you got so dizzy that you had to lie down on the floor for fear that you might fall down. You also said that you might mess on yourself and the floor. I told you not to worry about that. Then you told me that you were fine and not to worry about you. You said that you just had to go through this hardship, so I agreed and left you to your process.

"About a half hour later, you called out to me again, telling me how cold you were. You asked me to wrap you in blankets."

"I did? I don't have any recollection of that!"

"After I wrapped you, you said you were fine and you asked to be left alone again."

"Amazing! I have zero memory of that."

"Then, just about ten minutes ago, you called out again to ask for warm water because you were dehydrated, so I made some and brought it here in a thermos, and that's when you looked at me and sat up."

"And you have been here recapping the experience with me since then?"

"Yes, that's right."

I had no recollection of our interactions during the time that I was in the bathroom. As strange as the experience was, the only thing that mattered was the palpable feeling of being deeply loved and supported. It just felt so indescribably good knowing that she had taken such care of me. I glowed with love.

"Weren't you scared?" I said.

"Not so much. I was worried at first, but you told me that you had taken the mushrooms and that you were having a powerful vision. You've had many visions over the years, so I trusted what you said."

"In retrospect," I said, "That wasn't me that asked you to leave. I don't think I was in control of my mouth in that moment. If I had been in control, I would have asked you to stay. I was being tormented by a demon, and that demon wasn't finished with me.

"During those periods of torment, I couldn't speak. I thought that I might be dead or even insane. But I wasn't as concerned about that as I was about you, and how you would be without me. I was so worried about what might happen to you. Would you be able to survive? Would you be happy? Would you be able to fall in love again? I just want you to be happy."

"I am happy," she said. "Don't worry about that." Then she made a joke:"Besides, I'm sure I will die before you, so don't worry about me."

"I'm glad you can joke at a time like this. But seriously, I was worried, and not just about you, but also my promise to Jesus. I need to get the book published. Life is so fleeting, as our young cousin just proved; we shouldn't waste any time. If I die before the book gets published, it will be a terrible regret."

As she ran me a bath, she said, "You know what's really strange? You never did soil yourself. Don't you feel like going to the toilet? Don't you feel sick at all?"

"Wow. I forgot all about that. No, my stomach feels fine, and I don't feel like I need to use the toilet at all ... so strange."

As she left the bathroom, I got in the bath to rest and recover, thermos of warm water at the ready. As I lay there, I could feel my nervous system and my cells making corrections. When there was something blocking the feeling of Oneness, the effect was noise within the body resulting in some sort of disruptive feeling or thought. When love shone through unimpeded, then there was blissful silence. I realized that the awakening process was not just an abstract idea. It was biological!

Once the psychedelic trip was completely finished, I got out of the bath and checked the time. The entire process lasted just over four hours. During the experience, time was so distorted that some points in the trip seemed to last days, months, years, even forever.

As painful as this experience was—maybe the most painful experience of my life—it was well worth the suffering, for I had seen the hidden disharmonies within that had tainted the very foundations of my life. I had new direction and clarity.

The psychic pain that I was forced to experience seemed to have an unexpected benefit of burning off a great deal of inner disharmony. I was beaming with insight and inspiration. I had prayed to see my remaining darkness, and my prayer was answered. I then understood the nature of the self, disharmony, and how it all comes from Oneness and love. What a blessing!

CHAPTER 9

behind revelation

The next day was Ethan's memorial service. I woke up feeling as if my body had just come through a horrible flu. I was thrashed. There were broken blood vessels around my eyes; my body drooped from extremely low blood pressure and exhaustion, creating the feeling that my consciousness was located at the bottoms of my feet. I was also in severe pain. During the trip, the pressure in my digestive system was so extreme that it blew up hemorrhoids the size of a tangerine. It was excruciatingly painful to move, let alone sit.

After the memorial service, I gave my condolences to the family. My aunt, Ethan's grandmother, said I looked terrible and that maybe I should see a doctor. I told her I would be fine, and then I passed on Ethan's message: "Be happy—no excuses."

She said through her tears, "I know that's what he would say. I'm trying ... it's so hard."

"I know. I know exactly what you mean." We hugged.

After the memorial service my wife and I headed straight home, due to my condition. I told my wife about the hemorrhoids. They were an ongoing issue and had flared up badly during my ayahuasca experience, but now they were even more extreme.

As a practitioner of healing arts, I wanted to heal them without relying on anyone else. Until that time, I hadn't realized it was pride, backed by the feeling of unworthiness, which was preventing me from seeking help. But once so much negativity had burned away, it was obvious that a psychological hurt had been preventing me from seeking help. With that awareness, I set up an appointment to see my doctor. I was not going to feed the inner demon of pride anymore.

My doctor took a look and grimaced. "Yep, those have to come off." He scheduled surgery for me as quickly as possible. Fortunately, one of his previous surgery patients canceled, and he was able to fit me into his schedule in just a few days.

I never thought I could be so happy about having surgery. But it was such a relief to set aside the oppressive pride, the thought of surgery was actually pleasing. "Just grab your chainsaw and go at it," I joked.

The surgery went well. I didn't feel a thing. It's so strange how you go into the surgery room conscious, and you start chatting with the anesthesiologist, and in the next second you're being told that surgery is done—no pain, no nothing, until ...

A few hours later, I was feeling it. The doctor prescribed a heavy-duty painkiller called oxycodone, warning me that it could be highly addictive, and that I should use it for only a few weeks, according to directions. I told the nurse that I probably wouldn't use it. She didn't believe me. She was right.

The pain was so severe that it caused cramps that began in my buttocks and ran all the way down my legs into my feet. I ended up taking the oxycodone and the extra-strength Tylenol that they also prescribed.

I spent my days lying on my stomach on the floor, in agony but trying to take as little of the pain meds as possible. The problem with such a strategy is that once you are in enough pain to motivate you to take painkillers, you have to suffer for quite a while as you wait for the body to assimilate the medication.

Fortunately for me, my wife agreed with my strategy and was there to give me massages a few times a day. That helped me to take the medicine less than I would have otherwise been required to do. I can only imagine what it must be like for people who don't have access to powerful painkillers and loving massages.

Since the pain was likely to continue for weeks according to my surgeon, I took this time as opportunity to practice not creating suffering, not creating negativity, and not mentally resisting the pain.

To begin with, I paid close attention to my habitual reaction to the severe pain, making note of the pattern. Describing my reaction would require writing a number of obscenities, so I will leave it to the reader's imagination regarding the words that may have escaped my lips.

I decided to make a pain protocol. No matter the degree of pain, I was not going to create any narrative about it. The rule was to directly experience the pain without trying to define it in any way. I also made it a goal to not tighten my breathing but, instead, to try to keep my breathing flowing through the pain.

My protocol did very little, if anything, to stop the pain, but—and this is very important—it did a lot for my mental health. I was much more in the present with the pain, with fewer attempts to mentally avoid it through imagination. Due to less mental and emotional turmoil, I wasted a lot less energy during the pain, and after the pain was over, my mind was able to move on without trying to dwell on the experience.

One of the effects of this new approach was that anxiety about the next round of pain lessened tremendously. I knew the pain would come and go, and there was little that I could do about it, other than taking pain medication, so I accepted the pain as best as I could while being careful not to take too many painkillers.

Once the hemorrhoids had healed sufficiently, I no longer needed to take oxycodone, and once I stopped taking it my body began sweating profusely. Even in the short time that I had used oxycodone, my body had accumulated enough of it that it took two full days of heavy sweating to normalize. Dangerous stuff to be sure.

That said, I was thankful to oxycodone for helping me to get through the pain. I was also thankful to the mushrooms for showing me the cause of my hemorrhoids and how that cause was related to my base disharmony, resistance to life. Let me explain.

Even as a young child I would sit on the toilet for great lengths of time because of constipation. I had occasional pain and itching down there, and, in retrospect, I am sure it was hemorrhoids. It was always that way, so I never thought anything of it. I assumed the itch and pain were normal.

I used to have a lot of stomachaches and abdominal cramps. I had constipation almost constantly. All of these symptoms were the result of my disharmonious mental/emotional state.

It would be easy to get upset at the visionary process for the tremendous suffering and pain that it brought up, but by then I understood the larger picture. I felt only appreciation.

I got to see my inner disharmony, correct my feeling and thinking, and keep my promise to Jesus by correcting my manuscript and then publishing it as *The Unbound Soul* several months later.

I was also able to keep my promise to my wife by loving and caring for her more completely than ever before, which was greatly magnified as it reflected back from her.

After all, what are a night of insanity and a month of agonizing pain in the end?

CHAPTER 10

the nexus point

Just about a year after that first mushroom experience, I felt the pull to take another psilocybin journey. This time I acquired 5 grams, another "heroic dose," of dried mushrooms to take on an empty stomach. I was directed to prepare the mushrooms in the same way as before, via a 20-minute simmering, while in silent meditation. When the mushrooms were ready, I poured the contents into a cup and went into my training room for my trip. The space had a nice atmosphere and was quite warm from the wood stove fire that I had prepared earlier.

I placed the cup next to me as I sat before the kamidana, which is a small Shinto shrine that is a traditional element of Japanese martial art schools. As is formal tradition, I bowed to the little house. Then I sat in silence until my body was pulled to reach for the brew. I prayed to go further in the process that began in the first journey, to work on any remaining issues that needed correcting.

As I sat before the shrine, the admonition "True martial arts begin and end with respect" came to mind. I made note of that thought, for it was not of my bidding. Was I about to receive a lesson in respect?

I turned off the light and enjoyed the shadows created by the flame of the wood stove, as I waited for the right time to drink the tea. About ten minutes passed before my arm reached for the tea. The cup was held close to my chest for a few minutes. Finally, my hand raised the cup to my lips.

I was expecting that I would consume all contents of the cup as had happened in the first ceremony, but my hand removed the cup from my lips after only taking half the liquid, a moderate dose. I consumed none of the mushrooms.

There arose the thought that maybe this trip was going to be a light one, but an inner knowing immediately quashed that thought. This trip was going to be every bit as powerful as the last. Within 15 minutes, the effects began. At first there was a light buzzing feeling around my body that then became audible. After a minute, the buzzing was accompanied by an orange hue to the room. Another minute later an ominous feeling came over my body. The trickster was upon me.

Out of nowhere a feeling arose that my body was going to kill itself. Let me be clear, the feeling was not mine. I sensed that it was the trickster's plan to kill me once he had full control over my body.

At first, I tried to dismiss the feeling, but the feeling only grew stronger as the mushrooms worked their way further into my system. The overwhelming power of the Trickster was coming on so quickly that I feared I would soon be unable to resist.

My eyes, of their own accord, looked at the billowing flames in the wood stove. I could hear the Trickster's laugh. I saw an image of my body pulling out a burning log to set the house aflame. "My god, if I don't get away from the wood stove, not only will I die, but so will my wife!" I thought.

With the concentrated force of my will, I forced my body to its feet and out the door, away from the fire. I staggered back to the house. I entered the living room to find the wood stove there ablaze and no one around. My eyes narrowed on the flame, as the power of the trickster surged. The pull to burn down the house grew stronger. I forced my eyes away from the flame and willed my body down the hall toward the safety of my bedroom. There was nothing dangerous inside it.

My wife was in the bathroom. As I passed by, I told her about the suicidal compulsion, and the fear that I might lose the tenuous control that I had over my body, for it was the only thing preventing suicide. I told her that I was going into the bedroom, and that for no reason should she let me come out, unless she was there to monitor me. She agreed.

I lay down on the carpet between the bed and dresser, so as to give my body as little space to move as possible. Determined to stay put, I pulled a quilt over my body to keep warm and closed my eyes.

Fortunately, upon closing my eyes, the trip deepened such that my body was immobilized. I was so dizzy and physically disoriented that I became sure my body was going nowhere. With that awareness, I relaxed into the experience.

A wind kicked up within my body, and I was ripped away, transported to another location and into another body. My body appeared to disassemble, pixel by pixel, before being swept away into some nonformed, rapidly moving space, before being digitally reformed as another body.

Suddenly I was entirely someone else in every sense of the word, with no memory of Richard. It was as if my spirit liquefied and poured into another cup to then take on the dimensions of that cup.

I was an older teen in simple exploration of his world. I was lying on the floor next to a door at a party. I could hear other teens directing comments at me. I could hear one girl say in a worried tone, "Are you okay?" Then a boy said, "Leave him alone, he's fine. Just calm down. He's fine!" I, as that boy, had also taken some psychedelic substance and was tripping hard.

After a short while, a powerful force began to press upon me. Then I was sucked out of that body and pulled through some sort of inner space, away from that life. I thought I was going to hell. I feared that I would never return. It was utterly terrifying because I was that boy and I was being pulled away from all that I had ever known, from the people and the life that I loved. I tried to grab onto my body psychically, but I wasn't strong enough. My spirit unzipped slowly and painfully. There was so much fear—hell!

Then my perception, little by little, reassembled from this other dimensional space as Richard—but I could remember being that other person. And with that memory, I realized that my life experience as "a spiritual teacher" was no more special than was my life experience as that boy. While this observation seems an obvious one that I may have felt, considered, and even taught many times before, this time because I had actually perceived being someone else, the realization ran much deeper.

No life is any more valuable than any other. It is all just as it is. A thought arose: "Surely there is something special about my life. After all, I have dedicated myself to finding truth. Isn't that worth something?"

Then the presence of the Trickster was fully upon me, filling my body up from within with its demonic power. "Truth! Ha! You think you know the truth! Arrogant! So arrogant! What truth do you think you know?"

The demon began pulling up my beliefs one by one, and as each belief arose into thought, I was sucked into the world of that belief, its implications, hypocrisy, and suffering. It was as if I was walking through a maze generated by the belief, only to reach the full maturity of that belief and the suffering that it created before I found myself back in my body, feeling arrogant and false.

In the maze, no matter how I tried to justify the belief, doing so only led me into still more suffering, until I fully admitted the belief was false.

Having my cherished beliefs utterly crushed through the experience of their full bloom felt horrible. The cleverer were my justifications, the deeper and more prolonged was the suffering, a suffering that spread to the world around me to negatively affect other people's quality of life.

As soon as I admitted the disaster of one belief, yet another belief arose, and off I went, back into the maze. The amount of suffering my beliefs were causing in the world was gut-wrenching, and how foolishly arrogant I was in my attempts to justify those beliefs.

I began to repent. It didn't help. Another philosophy or "My Truth" arose, and off I went again, and again, and again, and again ... forever.

All this was good fun for the trickster, who was sure to accuse me with each return from the maze of ego. I realized that any thought I held as a truth was just a dream masquerading as truth. Regardless of the apparent virtue of any particular philosophy or ideology, I realized that clinging to any of them led to suffering. I realized that all ideologies are born of fear and the desire to feel in control.

Eventually the pool of beliefs was spent, and I found my perception back in my body. I noticed that it was moving on its own to release the bound-up energy of those beliefs. The body would stretch this way and that. There were powerful adjustments in the ankles, knees, hips, spine, neck, and arms. The release of this bound energy felt wonderful.

Once the adjustments were finished, I noticed that my left hand began moving to form a cross just in front of my face. The energy of the cross projected into the core of my brain. As the movement progressed, I felt as if data were downloading into the unconscious to be revealed at a later time.

As the download continued, in my mind's eye, an inner light gradually built into a brilliant flare that enveloped me to burn away the energy of self-judgment. This painful experience caused my brain and nervous system to ache. The burning seemed to go on, and on, and on.

After what seemed like days, the burning subsided. I could see that the cross my left hand had drawn in front of my face now overlaid the world. The horizontal plank of the cross represented the technological advancements of society based on the culture's founding beliefs, while the vertical bar represented the correction process that ultimately brings down civilizations in apocalypse.

As a civilization advances, based on some idea of truth, the horizontal plank lengthens to represent complexity, structure, and wealth. Great artwork and technology arises during this time, but eventually the society runs into the limitation of the ideology, which shows up as vice and ever-weakening human spirit resulting from too much comfort and insulation from reality. Unquestioning minds lead people, ever more gradually, out of sync with nature. As they lose sync they begin, more and more, to sacrifice integrity for short-term gain and ease. It is as if people become spiritually hollowed out. Nothing seems to fulfill or satisfy them. They are like hungry ghosts consuming everything in sight.

As people become increasingly disconnected and self-centered, wealth accumulates into the hands of a few, leaving the majority in poverty, and with that the sense of community is lost. Laws increase exponentially in an effort to force cohesion in a community-less society, and to maintain the existing power structure. By this time the society is running on pure momentum, largely devoid of love, with the demonic strumming of "My Truth" as background music. The founding ideologies of society have so thoroughly failed that few in the community live in accordance with it.

As the sense of community grows still weaker, corruption takes root, the people fracture into ideologically opposed groups, debt soars, and extremism grows, inevitably leading to war, famine, and disease.

I saw that once society reaches this stage, where we are now, one or more wise individuals, who see the big picture, attempt to awaken society. But, regardless of such individuals, society rots, knocking humanity into a more primitive lifestyle for a time. Ultimately the "truth" that gave rise to civilization brings about its demise.

Before the horizontal plank of the cross reaches the

70

limits of its founding ideology, opportunity exists for individuals in society to open themselves to wisdom, to see beliefs and ideologies as the demonlike, soul-possessing forces that they are and thereby awaken from puppetlike unconsciousness.

Contrasting the mindset of the majority is that of a handful of awakening individuals, who see the corrective forces as great opportunities to reflect and refine perception. These individuals tend to see the cause-and-effect relationship between beliefs and the self-serving disconnect of humanity that paves the path of suffering. Such individuals tend to abandon civilization just before it's too late, preferring, instead, to live a simple life in tune with nature. Society collapses.

The vision showed that over periods of hundreds or thousands of years, tribes of awakening individuals live simple, relatively balanced lives in communities, with minimal technological advancement.

Slowly population density rises, and gradually tribes begin amalgamating into larger groups, wherein individuals lack sufficient personal relationships with the majority of their tribe for the simple reason that one person just can't keep meaningful, trusting relationships with more than a few hundred people simultaneously. Rifts begin to build and smaller groups split away to seed new societies.

At some stage the force of ideology and belief takes over again, separating the burgeoning populations into opposing forces and eventually leading to fearsome arms races that stimulate technological advancement—so the horizontal bar grows.

Again, sophistication takes root, leading to a lifestyle of insulation, convenience, and lack of harmony with nature. Gradually the culture grows too far out of sync with nature to remain viable. Another correction occurs—apocalypse.

I saw that there have been many such corrective cycles, each lasting hundreds or sometimes thousands of years. So much war, so much suffering, and the loss of so much knowledge has accompanied each cycle. It just seemed so pointless. But what was most disturbing was the thought that this cycle would continue until humans were completely wiped from the planet. Within the vision I speculated that this condition would continue until another species evolved to play the same ideological game. Considering that our society has nuclear weapons, human extinction seemed the inevitable conclusion, barring some miracle.

Initially I thought that the horizontal growth represented by ideology and technological advancement was good, but after seeing the cycle multiple times, the pattern of mass corruption became clear. So I began to favor the simpler, more "primitive" lifestyle that was more in tune with nature.

But after viewing the whole cycle enough times, I began to realize that even the "primitive" lifestyle was flawed because it ultimately led right back into advancement and on to yet another correction.

I began to see through the illusion that my mind was creating, which was that these two planks were opposing forces. I could see that they were but opposite sides of one circle, in that, ultimately, one curves exactly into the other, given sufficient time. I could see that instead of two separate forces, this cycle was more like the seasons—winter moves into summer which leads back into winter, endlessly.

Various cultural symbols began flashing into my mind. The cross became the Buddhist swastika, with its cross spinning, which represented the cycle of suffering, the maze of ego. The swastika morphed into the Taoist yin and yang symbol, to then become the mathematical symbol for infinity, which then became the ouroboros, the serpent that circles to eat its own tail. All of these symbols represented the maze of ego and the cycle of suffering. Through the myriad morphing of symbols, I saw that they all represented the same thing, a warning from the deep unconscious that has been passed down through the ages in all corners of the world. The irony of these symbols is that many of them were ultimately incorporated into the very ideologies that they warned about.

Motivated by ideology, humanity unconsciously moves through the maze of ego and the cycle of suffering, and each step takes us ever closer to what we wish to avoid—suffering. I saw that the very same ideological sickness that the trickster had used to punish me with was at the heart of cultures worldwide.

I then thought, "Maybe this cross, in this vision, represents a natural phenomenon, not something deserving of condemnation. Maybe ideology is natural." It was a miserable thought because, to me, it meant that endless suffering was unavoidable.

I saw the cycle repeat multiple times, and with each cycle, my hand redrew a cross over my forehead. The tempo of the movement increased as the vision cycled on, my hand moving ever faster. The manic tempo revealed the inherent insanity of this cycle. So much pain and suffering, so much lost each time!

"Why is the universe so cruel?" I wondered. "There has to be a better way, a way that allows for the advancement of society, while simultaneously enhancing people's sense of connection with each other and nature, a way that does not lead to corruption, a way that is in perpetual balance with all that is."

With that thought, my attention was drawn to the very center of the cross, and as I looked, a light began to grow out of the center point. As the light grew, rotating circles that represented ideas, beliefs, philosophies, and ideologies were linked together by the light of a central nexus point. The light from the nexus point of these circles grew ever larger until it enveloped the circles with its brilliance. The brilliance then filled me.

I could see, within my own life, the pattern of a cross—simplicity leading to complexity that then brings decay and subsequent correction. I saw life and death, life and death, from the largest galaxies to the smallest microorganism, the tempo increasing ever faster. Life, death, life, death, life, death.

My body tightened in resistance to a pressure that arose from within at a cellular level. It was an extraordinarily uncomfortable feeling, as if my body were being forced to accept something completely foreign to its programming. It felt as if I were witnessing an important evolutionary step while it was occurring within my body.

I saw that my friends, my family members, my wife, and everyone dear to me represented unconscious archetypes that served to structure my mind and dictate my path in society. I saw my cells and nervous system creating blips of mental noise that I can best describe as precursor thoughts and precursor emotions that bubble up from psychic imbalance and disturb awareness. I had experienced these precursor thoughts and emotions many times during my years of meditation. Precursors are unformed and unintelligible, until the mind grabs and strings them together with memory sequences to form meanings, full-blown images, stories, and narratives. When I saw them during meditation, it was from an objective perspective, but I realized that during states of lower consciousness, states of self-absorption, these sequences trapped perspective, directing it into unconscious, reactive patterns—the maze of ego and the cycle of suffering.

I realized that self was just an amalgamation of assumptions, biases, beliefs, associations, and strategies, born of these biological precursors that at best help the body survive the experience of life—and at worst lead to dysfunction.

I understood that, with a little insight and honesty, self is not seen as anything other than a tool that lets the body function in the world, like a label on a mailbox that allows for communication between people. When taken beyond function, self can be likened to a demon that possesses the soul and causes all manner of suffering and dysfunction at every turn.

Assumptions about myself began to crumble. I realized that everything I thought myself to be was just a function of memory, and memories are a subjective and unstable record of experience. I was reminded that I had no way to verify my existence. My entire life could be a figment of the imagination. I found it sad to think that I might have never existed, but it was even sadder when I realized that the very same thing could be said of everyone I had ever known or loved.

There is simply no way to prove that anything we sense, remember, or value is, or ever was, real. The entire thing could be an illusion. Even more disheartening was the realization that every "choice" I had made could have simply appeared to be a choice when "I" made it. But if there is no self, then choice starts to become a bit rabbit-holey.

Ego wanted to assert that I had chosen my life, that I had decided to do one thing or another, but I could see that before "I" had consciously chosen anything, there was already a precursor deep down that was in alignment with the choice that I thought I had consciously selected, which indicated that the choice was made before "I" had even become aware of it. The experience of choosing was only the bubbling up of something that was already decided. What this meant was that "I" could not honestly take credit for any of the content of "my life story."

Suddenly everything that I thought I knew was

highly questionable. The effect was horrifying—at first. But the more that I saw it, the more I began to relax, and the more I relaxed, the more I realized that not knowing was okay, even healthy—vibrantly healthy.

It then became clear that the entire experience of life might be like a story with no author. If there is no self then this entire experience is just as it is—no one is in control. Life is like a giant river meandering to the ocean. In such a case, even the realization that life has no author is nothing special, just a part of the flow, and something the individual can't rightly take credit for.

To say that the self exists is to take a position outside the nexus point, to suffer. But, conversely, to say that the self does not exist is also to step out of the nexus point and into suffering.

Then I understood what this vision was showing me. When society exists at the center point of the cross, then and only then will the cycle of suffering end. Being at that center point is just as important for society as it is for the individual. To exist at the center—or as I saw it, the nexus point amid infinite circles—is to observe both being and nonbeing with equal attentiveness, appreciating mind and presence equally, valuing both form and being, duality and nonduality, knowledge and innocence, for it is all part of what *is,* but none of it is true in and of itself.

I was reminded of that teenage boy whose body I entered at the beginning of the trip, and I remembered how much he loved his life, and how he was clearly having "a bad trip." I realized that every life, even without "bad trips," has sufficient suffering to feed inner demons. I certainly had plenty of suffering in my life, and that kid whose body I had entered had his. All life has experienced hardship in the process of surviving, so everyone deserves a little respect simply for existing, no matter how disagreeable or silly the person may be. After all, I could find myself in anyone's body, and any of them could be in mine, as the trip had demonstrated.

The mushrooms were done with me, and I awoke from the trip, clear and thankful simply for being. I immediately rose and walked out to greet my wife, just as sober as if I had not taken the mushrooms. Usually the comedown of a psilocybin trip is gradual, but this one just ended. I looked at the clock and discovered that the total time for this trip was just about three hours.

Afterward I enjoyed a hearty meal as I pondered the experience.

CHAPTER 11

the war within

My final psilocybin trip took place just a few months later. I was drawn to simmer a surprisingly small amount of mushroom, probably about 1 gram, for 20 minutes. One gram of dried mushroom is usually insufficient for a "mystical experience," but this time a small dose felt correct.

While the tea simmered, I remained in silence, waiting for any prayers or question to arise. After some time a question emerged: "What is the cause of inner division? How can human beings heal this division and live Oneness?"

I drank only about half of the liquid before my body told me to stop. The dosage was so low that it was hard to imagine that it could produce a mystical experience. An inner knowing indicated that I had consumed exactly the right amount.

This time I was careful to start my journey in my bedroom, a place free of fire. As with the two previous psilocybin trips, the effects came on within about 15 minutes, starting with a tingling in my blood, and an orange tint to the visual field.

In retrospect, I may be highly sensitive to psilocybin. For my body, the effects may be multiple times what they would be for the average consumer. When I took the "Heroic dose" of 7.5 grams during my first trip, I may have had the effect of 15 grams or more. While 15 grams may seem to be really dangerous, there are people who have worked their way up beyond 30 grams without compromising their health. As sensitivities to psilocybin vary from person to person, it is best to set aside expectations initially. You will know after the trip is over.

I turned off the light and laid myself on the bed to relax into the process. After a few minutes, I could feel the ominous presence of the trickster in the room. A sinking feeling came over me with the sudden awareness that he was out to kill me again. I had forgotten that I had a razor sharp katana (samurai sword) in my closet. A vivid image came to mind of my body retrieving the sword, unsheathing it, and turning the tip toward my abdomen before my body sank onto it.

The effects of the psilocybin were coming on

strong, and I knew if I did not eliminate access to the weapon, I was done for. I strongly felt that going into the closet to remove the weapon would turn out badly. Just touching that sword was going to be more than I could resist.

Fortunately that closet has a lock on it, and I had the key on my nightstand. Quickly, I got up, grabbed the key, and dizzily walked to the closet to lock it. After locking the door, I threw out the keys, into the dark hallway, and shut the bedroom door behind me. I made my way back to the bed, knowing that I would soon be too incapacitated to move at all. With that thought, the ominous feeling vanished.

A powerful wind whisked me away with a tornado-like roar. My body digitally unzipped, and I disappeared into the abyss. The next thing I knew, I was in the body of someone else, a little boy who was sitting alone on a living room sofa at midday, daydreaming. I had no recollection of myself as Richard. I was just a bored daydreaming boy. The experience of that boy was just as normal as is the perception of daily reality for anyone. The only odd thing about the room was the 1980s décor. In retrospect, I may have "time-traveled."

I was that child for several minutes before the wind kicked up again to suck me away. As that boy, I had no recollection of Richard, or that I was on a psilocybin journey. I had no prior knowledge of the wind. I was just a boy being ripped from his body, feeling that I would never return. I tried with all my might to hold on, but I couldn't. I was pulled out of my body from behind. I willfully latched onto the top of the couch. Then I was the top of the couch. I became the fabric of the couch covering. I could perceive the room from the perspective of the fabric where my perception was holding. I had no memory of being the boy or of being Richard. All I knew was the perspective of the fabric.

The wind surged, and I tried to hold onto my identification as the fabric. I was terrified to lose my perception, my reality, for it was all I ever knew. Ever so slowly, I was pulled out of that perception, despite my will to hold on. To be ripped away from my perception as the fabric and into the hell of the dark unknown was horribly fearful.

I found my perception back in the body of Richard. I could remember the simple, mundane, but magical life of that child. It was good. I could remember being the fabric. It was good, too. Each time my perception was pulled out, I was terrified of losing myself. Those perceptions, in retrospect, were equally important to me, for each set was all that I knew at the time.

My body began to move on its own to stretch and release bound-up energy. It felt fantastic. My left hand rose to my forehead, just as it had in the previous trip, and redrew a cross. Then my forefinger pointed to the bridge of my nose, between my eyes, just below the skull ridge. A voice in my head said, "Here." My hand redrew the cross, and then my finger pointed again to the same spot. "Here," the voice repeated. As the hand drew, I noticed that the very center of the cross was the one point that my finger had indicated. Again, the voice in my head said, "Here."

"Remember this point," the voice said. "It is vital."

Suddenly my body stood and walked robotically to the bathroom to urinate. There was no me, just the body moving of its own accord.

Once it flushed the toilet, my body began shaking to move out energy. It would shake for a minute, and then the forefinger would rise to touch the point before shaking again.

I could feel precursor thoughts and emotions arising to form intelligible thought. What emerged was a long held belief, weaker than it was in the last journey, but still there. In a flash, I found myself in the maze of ego. I remembered having this same experience in the last trip, and it was no fun. I thought I had already learned this lesson, but not deeply enough, it seemed.

I could see the ramifications of the belief taken to full maturity through totally realistic experience. I got to experience the suffering that the belief created for me and the world. When I reached the pinnacle of suffering that the belief fueled, the experience ended. The main difference between this experience of the maze and that of the previous trip was that this time I had no inclination to justify the beliefs that arose. My perception returned to the darkness of my mind.

"The naked arrogance, the audacity!" My accuser, the trickster, was back. I could feel my rapid descent into hell. "You are so full of yourself! You think you are wise. Arrogance!"

I was dumbstruck with confusion. The descent into hell seemed to come out of nowhere. More precursors bubbled up, into the window of perception, before instantly forming into thought, into another "truth." I was back in the maze of ego, watching as that truth wound its way through all sorts of suffering before ending up right back in the self, the ego.

I could feel myself dropping still deeper into hell, amid the trickster's ongoing laughter. Suddenly, in mid-fall, it occurred to me: These precursor thoughts and feelings are bubbling up from the nervous system. They are biological in origin. The very perception of self is biological. It is just the body doing what is habitual. There really is no one to blame. I am not guilty of arrogance, because the self is just a biological construct. Who could possibly be to blame?

With that realization the maze of ego vanished, and my perception rose out of hell. My body stretched and adjusted to move out the energy. My finger pointed to the location between my eyes." Here, here, here," it stressed, again and again. "Do not forget this point!" It felt as if one part of the brain was trying to get the message through to other parts.

A biological fear seemed to exist that the point would be forgotten, for a great deal of what occurs during visions is lost from memory upon return to normal waking awareness, much like forgetting a dream.

Thoughts and feelings began to bubble up and take form again, and I was back in the maze. The trickster cackled. I was just into the maze, and beginning to see the ramifications of a belief, when self-blame arose. It was then that I remembered these thoughts were biological and there was no self to blame.

The realization that there was no one to blame empowered and freed my perception. I could see how the very interest in awakening, which began when I was a child, was an upwelling from my nervous system. I had not chosen to awaken because there was no "I" to choose. The very pull to consume the mushroom tea was also biological, as was each and every thought and feeling that "I" had ever had. Even the belief that there was or was not a self was biological. If all these things were biological, then that also implied that the trickster was also a biological effect. With insight, I realized that the trickster no longer had sufficient power over my perception to pull it back into the maze.

The trickster disappeared, to be replaced by an angelic being. "Richard's body has learned the lesson of the mushroom. To take the mushroom again would unnecessarily burden the body without further benefit. Take no more."

I found my body standing in the middle of the bathroom, moving out energy. "Here, here, here," my body repeated, pressing my finger ever harder between my eyes, to the point that it was becoming somewhat painful.

"*Here!*"

Finally, there arose an awareness that my body had so thoroughly incorporated the feeling that the brain was sure it would remember, even after the trip was finished.

My body turned to the bathtub and began filling it with hot water. Without a thought, it exited the bathroom and went into the bedroom to lie on the bed.

As I lay there, I could feel two entities within, one angelic, benevolent, the other demonic, malevolent. The angelic entity was the force of love, while the malevolent entity, the trickster, was at war with the angelic entity to control the body and perception.

The trickster wanted total control, and he demanded respect, and if he could not get the respect that he demanded, he would use whatever control over the body he could muster to kill that body.

I realized what was happening. My body had awakened to the point where love was now on equal footing with the power of the trickster and rapidly moving beyond the trickster's control. Love was no longer submissive to fear, a balance that greatly threatened the trickster's authority. I saw that this battle was taking place between the two hemispheres of the brain. The left represented the trickster, and the right represented the angel.

The trickster was putting up his best fight. My perception would shift from the left hemisphere, the spirit of malevolence, to the right hemisphere, the spirit of benevolence, and back again. When in benevolence, there was peace, gratitude, and openness. When in malevolence, there was the demand for respect, for control, for power.

As benevolence grew still more powerful, the words "Damn you!" and "God damn you!" came out of my mouth. "If I'm going to lose my power, I am not going down without a fight. I will do this properly and fight to my very last breath, God damn it!"

With those words, my body rose from the bed,

went back to the bathroom and shutoff the water, which was at just the right height and temperature. My body stripped off all clothing, turned to the toilet, and released its bladder. The shining, magical glow of the mushroom's essence was clearly visible in the water. My body bowed deeply to the spirit of psilocybin and flushed the toilet before turning to formally enter the bathtub.

Unexpectedly, words came from my lips. "In honor of the great unification, we show respect through ceremony," the trickster said. My body kneeled in the bathtub and bowed to the universe. "The two unite to be one whole—holy," he said. My body lay back in the warm water. A moth landed on the edge of the bathtub, right next to me, and seemed to bow. My eyes focused on it, and it seemed to have died. The focus of my eyes emitted such raw power that it killed the moth.

"Oh, we can't have that," said the transforming voice of the trickster as he unified, little by little, with the angelic spirit. I could feel the brain hemispheres energetically unifying. And as they came together, a power in my body grew to miraculous, but untempered proportions. Raw power had killed the moth. My hand reached out, forefinger touching the moth. The moth tilted onto its side, unmoving, dead as dead. "Come back" my voice said, and my forefinger touched the moth again before moving away to give the moth space. Still it did not move. "Come back," my voice repeated, and my finger touched the moth again. A power moved into it, and it flittered away, alive and well.

In a flash the sense of me returned. I wondered, "Did that really happen?" Just as quickly, self was gone again. My right hand rested on my heart to feel its powerful pulse. There the hand remained for about a minute, in tune with the calm, powerful beating. Then, suddenly, the pulse disappeared. It seemed that my heart had stopped, although my body glowed with life. The sense of "I" popped back onto the scene for a flash and wondered, "Has my body died?" With that, the ego vanished, to be replaced by a mental count to 60—one minute. The heart never moved. Breathing, however, never fully stopped, although it was barely detectable, so thin was it.

The understanding arrived that the body was resetting itself, to begin again with a fresh perspective. The heart resumed beating as normal. With that, my body rose from the bath, toweled off, dressed, and went back to the bedroom to lie down again.

As soon as the body lay down, a vision began. I could see that first one person would unify, and from the power of that unification, many other individuals would also unify to end the war within and find true peace. When the war within ends for enough people, so too would peace come to the external world.

Back in bodily awareness, my mouth cursed repeatedly: "Fuck, fuck, fuck, fuck you all! Fuck the world!"

"I" wondered why the trickster was still cursing. Was he not yet fully united with his other half, the Angel?

"No, it is not complete, and as promised, I am

going to do this right! I will fight to the very last breath of me. Fuck you!"

Again, my body rose from the bed and returned to the bathroom, stripped, and ceremonially reentered the water. Self returned. Looking down at the bottom of the bathtub, I could see tiny, hexagonal shapes overlaying the physical structure of the tub. Looking around the room, I could see the same pattern everywhere. The visual field still had an orange tint to it as well, so I knew I was still tripping.

The unification of my body brought about a deep, penetrating silence and the feeling of incredible power. My body and intention had become a tremendous force of nature. There was no self, no thought, and no emotion, just penetrating clarity.

Then came the realization that this way of being could be permanent if I chose it. It was time to make a choice.

An image of my wife came to the fore. I realized that I had largely lost the capacity for personal love. And that the choice for unification, at this stage of my life, would erase all possibility for intimate human interaction.

I realized that without personal love I would not be able to fulfill my promise to my wife—to love and care for her to the end of my days. Then there came the realization that personal love is not just for our strength but also for our frailty. Any loving parent would understand this feeling. Consider the love that you have for your children. Your love protects and nourishes them. They are precious to you, in large part, because of their frailty.

How could my wife have a personal relationship with a force of nature? It would be impossible for anyone. To the extent that my body unified, it had ceased to be human, at least with regard to what people love about humanity.

The power that shone through my body was so tangible and awe-inspiring that it would surely terrify most people. A choice had to be made, but it really wasn't a choice, for in that moment, there was no "me" to choose. My mouth uttered the "choice," and with that my body rose from the bath, toweled off, dressed, and went back into my bedroom to sleep, the story of my life to continue. The trip was over.

The next day I awoke, careful not to believe or disbelieve anything that had happened, for it was obvious that to do either would pull awareness out of the nexus point and into a "truth," which would lead to the maze of ego and all the suffering that it brings. No profound awareness was needed to see how clinging to something as a truth leads to imbalance.

To exercise his sadistic joy the trickster had used as a weapon the "truths" that my body clung to. As terrible as that experience was, I learned something valuable from it: that it was possible to live without clinging to thoughts and feelings.

I am not saying that thoughts and feelings are wrong. They simply are as they are. After all, the body needs some degree of belief even to move. If one did not believe that water would quench thirst, one would not drink.

Realizing that belief has its place is important. The imbalance comes when we cling to those beliefs as if they are ultimate truths. The same imbalance occurs when we blindly or arrogantly disbelieve things, because both assertion and denial are positions in the maze of ego, outside the nexus point.

Suffering is inevitable outside the nexus point. Does the nexus point represent a truth? No, but the model is functional, and that is enough. Any more weight given to the concept would result in dysfunction. To remain in balance, one avoids extremes and uses no more force than is necessary to accomplish anything, which I found to be very little force indeed for most things.

The same principle applies to beliefs. Minimize them to just enough for motivation, and keep them light and open-natured, so that they can change as your path of awakening progresses.

CHAPTER 12

the sage

I went through a period of months wherein I noticed my mind would bring up certain assumptions and "truths" unconsciously. Generally, after the fact, awareness of the transgression arrived, and so, little by little, the tendency faded away. I was careful not to place any belief in the content of the psychedelic experience beyond what it could do to improve the quality of my life and the world around me. If the body still held onto the concept of *savior*, surely it would have fallen into the "I'm special" trap, based upon the content of that last vision. Surely, over the course of humanity, many bodies have taken that bait to self-identify as "The Chosen One."

The perspective change provided by these visions proved quite useful to me, and I was clearly able to see the benefits in my life. My wife also saw that the experiences produced positive changes in my general outlook and attitude, even though she was originally opposed to my taking these substances. I found her admission that I had made clear progress by means of psilocybin to be validation of its efficacy, at least with regard to my awakening process.

A number of months passed before the next step connected to psychedelics arose within me. While researching this book, I came across a relatively new and lesser known substance, the pound-for-pound most naturally psychedelic substance known to science. *Salvia divinorum* is a plant in the mint family, specifically a form of sage. It grows naturally in Mexico, in the province of Oaxaca. The local natives, the Mazatec Indians, claim to have been using the sage ceremonially and for healing purposes since antiquity. Its Latinate name means "the diviner's sage."

After reading and documenting the available information on *Salvia divinorum*, I thought nothing more of it until several months later, when I drove into the parking lot of my meditation studio. Suddenly, I knew I needed to get some *Salvia divinorum*. I had only 15 minutes until class started, so there was no way for me to get any, but, clearly, I needed it right away. I did a quick internet search for smoke shops in the area, to see if any of them carried the substance. After all, it was totally legal in most states.

I found a shop just two blocks away that carried it. I called the shop and talked with the owner for a few minutes to inquire about the substance. He told me what they had available and that I would need a pipe and a torch lighter to smoke it, as *Salvia divinorum* needs to burn hot.

As I had no time to visit the shop, I called a student, Mark, to ask whether he could drop by the shop to purchase salvia, a pipe, and a torch lighter on his way to meditation class later in the evening. Mark was an adventurous sort, and he was happy to oblige.

Later that evening, Mark and another student, Donna, joined me for a brief introduction to the world of the sage. As it was the first time any of us had tried *Salvia divinorum*, we followed a specific protocol to assure that the tripping individual was safe. At all times, one of us had to be sober to watch over the others. Although salvia has an extremely good safety profile, with no record of anyone having ever died of overdose, people who resist it can be in for a hell of a ride, and sometimes they may panic and physically move around—a recipe for disaster.

Salvia was being sold at various degrees of potency. The lowest potency was five times more powerful than would be the natural dried leaf. Essentially, preparers extract the psychoactive substance, Salvinorin A, and then soak the dried salvia leaves in the concentration to increase the potency. At the shop where we purchased *Salvia divinorum*, the potencies range from five times to 50 times that of the natural dried leaf. I was clearly drawn to the quintuple potency, so that is what I requested the student to purchase.

I knew going into this process that smoked salvia has a very short window of peak psychedelic potency, generally about five minutes, with a quick comedown that tapers off usually 20 to 30 minutes after smoking it. To be safe, we set aside several hours for our introduction to *Salvia divinorum*. As my inner knowing instructed me that this session was only an introduction, I was only to take one smoke.

Salvia smells and tastes arguably similar to tobacco, and for people who cannot smoke, chewing the substance as a quid or taking it as a tincture may be more appealing. As I grew up in a smoker's household, smoking didn't seem to bother my lungs at all.

I took a full breath of the smoke and held it for a long time before releasing it. As soon as I released the smoke, I put the pipe down. In that instant, the room split in half visually, with the right side peeling away like the pages of an open book being flipped.

An ominous tricksterlike feeling came over me, and I could feel a wind kick up. There arose the distinct feeling that I was close to being pulled away. I knew this feeling well, for it was exactly what it felt like when the psilocybin sucked me out of my body.

The page flipping continued for a few minutes before the room returned to normal. The presence of the trickster was gone. My pores opened up with sweat as the compound was expelled from my body. I knew if I took a few more puffs, I would be swept away to who-knows-what.

I was feeling totally normal and natural within minutes of coming down from the peak. The total experience lasted just a few minutes. Compared to psilocybin, the liftoff was incredibly fast, after maybe 30 seconds, in my case. For me, psilocybin usually took 10 to 15 minutes for effects to begin, but for most people it would be somewhere between 30 minutes to two hours to start.

Once I came back, I briefly reported what I could of my experience before Mark and Donna took their puffs. Mark reported that smoking salvia made him feel euphoric. Donna had a brief traveling experience, wherein she described the room dividing, with one half of the room being upside-down above her. She found herself looking through the floorboards of a diner at a waitress, who was just above her. She felt eager to enter that room but was pulled back to her normal perception before she could go any further.

I questioned Mark about the euphoria he felt, and he described it as reminiscent of cocaine or MDMA (ecstasy). As I had never tried either of those drugs, I had nothing to hang the comparison upon. My experience was not euphoric at all, just a perception change and a little disorientation. I drove home feeling that I would be taking a heavy dose later that evening.

Upon arriving home, I told my wife of what had transpired and that I was going to have a ceremony that night in the bedroom. All that she asked was that I keep the bedroom windows open to air out the smoke.

I went into the bedroom, prepared the pipe, and waited in silence to see what prayer or question arose, if any. After a few minutes, my hand reached for the pipe, no questions, and no prayers. It felt right, so off I went on a salvia journey. My body took four heavy puffs, holding each deeply before exhaling. By the time the fourth was released, the ominous feeling was upon me as the room unzipped digitally, pixel by pixel, and I was pulled into the abyss.

I found myself on a street in the body of a little girl. It was a beautiful, warm, sunny, late spring morning. I was playing hopscotch with a number of my friends, some girls and some boys. We were having a great time. I was that girl. I forgot who Richard was. I was in a joyous state of childlike play, for I had a nice group of friends to play with. It was a wonderful and totally realistic childhood experience.

I had just reached the last chalked hopscotch square when the wind kicked up and began sucking me out of my body. I was a terrified little girl with no idea what was happening. I could feel the abyss that I was being pulled into, and it felt like utter hell. I was going to lose everything that I had ever known and loved. The sensation was awful. I psychically grabbed onto anything that I could. The wind was pulling me down and out the back of the body, through the asphalt. I manage to grab onto the asphalt. Then, suddenly, I was the asphalt.

A car drove slowly over me, and I could feel the pressure. It did not hurt, but it was surprising. Being asphalt felt totally normal and good. The wind kicked up again, and I was swept into the abyss in terror, away from all that I had ever known, an asphalt existence.

Suddenly, I was back in my body, feeling the wind still whisking across me. I could see the pixels of the world re-assimilate around my body, as the feeling of the trickster dissipated. The peak experience lasted 15 minutes, much longer than in a typical smoking trip.

Apart from the utter fear of being swept away, and the ominous feeling of the trickster at the very beginning and end of the trip, everything about the experience was entirely realistic. I was a kid, I was asphalt, and then I was Richard. The experiences of being someone or something else were totally realistic, and normal—nothing special, and nothing like imagination.

What was the lesson here, I wondered? I didn't like my reaction to the spirit-whisking transportation system and the abysslike dimensional doorway. The utter fear that being ripped out of my life stimulated, as well as the unexpected presence of the trickster, was something to look into, I thought.

It surprised me that salvia took me to exactly the same sort of experience as did psilocybin. They were entirely different chemicals, with no molecular similarities. While dimensional travel and becoming other people and things is commonly reported by salvia users, this phenomenon is not common to psilocybin. How on earth could these two vastly different chemical substances produce the very same effect, I wondered?

It seemed to me that both substances were stimulating the same brain-places, and none of it felt random or accidental. But what I was to learn from the salvia experience was not yet clear.

For some reason, I felt that I was on the verge of a powerful step forward in my awakening process. Despite my unpleasant experience with salvia, I felt that I would be doing it again before too long. I cleaned out the pipe, kissed my wife, and went to bed.

CHAPTER 13

facing fear

The recurrence of the trickster with *Salvia divinorum* got my attention. I spent the next day meditating on the fear that I had experienced while on salvia, for fear is the purview of the trickster, and his presence was a sign that I had a good lesson coming.

Through my meditation, I had several realizations. First, it was clear that, at least to some degree, I feared letting go of my life in exchange for falling into the unknown, which meant that the natural and only possible response, when getting pulled away, was resistance.

Then a thought arose: "The degree to which I loved my life was the degree to which I was unable to release." It was a strange thought that somehow felt not quite right. Then another thought arose: "Enlightenment is detachment." Again, there was something not quite right about the statement.

Living out the philosophy "Enlightenment is detachment" would preclude the possibility of personal love, for to be detached, as stated, meant that one could not embrace anything. This detachment was the very thing that my body felt when it unified in the final psilocybin trip.

My body had decided against this path for precisely the reason that it precluded the possibility of personal love. A feeling arose that unconditioned love should also include personal love, and my body was not yet fully ready for unification, as it still had other aspects to include for the unification to be holistic. Even if the previous vision was correct, and godlike power was achievable, without personal love, it would be uninspiring to others, and such a path would surely end with me.

According to the vision, unification would begin with one individual and then spread rapidly to others, resulting in a long period of true world peace. Without personal love in balance with universal love, the vision of world peace would be an impossibility, in my estimation, and that outcome would play right into the hands of the trickster, the master of suffering.

The trickster had promised to fight to the bitter end. Maybe the fight was still afoot within me, I thought. I felt strongly that I was right to reject "unification" when I did, for it was just another trap of the trickster, a false unification. Who would want godlike power without all facets of love to temper it? Only a sick person, I felt.

But a great many religions, especially ones that include monastic orders, hail detachment, which is why many of them disallow marriage. A close look at those particular orders shows that they are typically motivated by willpower and repression. For example, monks and nuns of those orders are not usually allowed to partake in sexual relations, marry, or by other means have a family. These rules sometimes result in uncontrollable urges, perversion, rape, and molestation. Detachment as a path and the resulting repression were clearly not suitable for human beings.

Furthermore, the frailty of the human body reveals as incomplete the philosophy of detachment. Due to the frailty of the human form, to survive, we are necessarily social creatures. We lack fur, claws, and sharp teeth, limitations that disallowed effective solo hunting for Stone Age human beings. The alternative to hunting is farming, which is also a group activity. Without the ability to hunt or farm, human beings can't handle temperature extremes because the regulation of body temperature requires sufficient caloric energy. Detachment precludes the ability to form sufficient social bonds that would allow for both hunting and farming.

Even with physical survival assured, detachment fails at a psychological level because the human animal starts to go insane when left alone for too long. We are not solitary creatures by nature. If we were, then solitary confinement would not be such an effective punishment in prisons. From accounts of prisoners, they fare better in the yard, with violent offenders, than they do in solitary confinement, even at the hardest prisons.

We need other people, and they need us. Personal relationships are vital, and you can't maintain a personal relationship unless you are invested in that relationship. After all, who would want to be friends with someone not invested in that friendship?

"What, then, is the right attitude towards life, a way of being that supports the people and the environment around us?" I wondered. Almost immediately after the question came to mind, the answer followed: "To simultaneously embrace and relinquish life fully in every moment."

The image of Tibetan monks making a mandala of sand came to mind. They dedicate days or even weeks to producing incredibly beautiful and intricate works of colored sand art. Then, once the mandala is complete, they wipe away the sand, utterly destroying the art. The sand mandala perfectly symbolizes the balance of full engagement and simultaneous release. I wondered whether the art form of making sand mandalas carried an ancient message down through the ages.

To me the message of the sand mandala was obvious. The way of harmony is to fully embrace and release life simultaneously. This answer felt vibrantly right. I realized that I needed to revisit the sage.

I spent the next few hours preparing myself for the possibility that I might never return from this trip. I realized that I could die, or go utterly insane, or maybe end up in hell, to be stuck there forever.

I determined that no matter the experience, whether psychedelic or not, from then on, I was going to fully embrace and release life in every moment. I figured that even if I found myself in hell, I would find a way of being that would make it a better place than it would otherwise be.

The words of my cousin Ethan came to mind: "Be happy—no excuses!" That's right, I thought. I will go with love, wherever I am taken.

With that, I knew it was time to begin my trip. I took six strong tokes before my body collapsed onto the floor. The powerful disintegration of the room was so disorienting that I had to close my eyes.

As soon as my eyes closed, I found that I was an older teenage boy. I was in a garage with my best friend and my cool uncle, looking at my newly bought used car. I was fully that boy, with no thought or memory of Richard. *In retrospect, judging from our clothing, the music, and the surroundings, it seems that I had traveled back in time.*

We continued car-talk for a few minutes before the wind kicked up and began to pull me out of the body. Although I did not remember the determination to fully embrace and release all of life through love, it seems, in retrospect that the determination had affected my experience as that boy. As the wind kicked up to unzip me from that experience, there was no fear; instead, a deep feeling of appreciation shone through me into the surrounding environment.

Suddenly, I remembered Richard and the intent of the trip that I was taking. A strong sense of rightness accompanied the attitude and the atmosphere that was created by that attitude. Everything was benefitting from the love in real way, and it reflected back at me harmonically. I found it amazing that I could be in that boy and also remember Richard.

The wind kicked up and pulled me into the metal of the garage door track. I was an atom of that track. I was happy that the people were happy. The experience was nice. The wind kicked up again, and I was pulled out of the atom and back into Richard's body.

As I entered Richard's body, there was a deep sense of joy in the room. I could feel that room itself was happy I was there. The atoms themselves were benefiting from the determination to love regardless of circumstance.

I awoke on the floor in my bedroom, feeling reborn. There was a strong pull to write, so I grabbed a piece of paper and wrote the following clumsy statements:

"I am awake. I am the center of all that is.

Each perspective is the center of all that is.

There is nothing better than to live a simple, happy life. There is no need for anything more. Simple lives of hugs, kisses, and generosity are everything. There is love, and there is the life born of that attitude. There is nothing profound about love. There is no great teaching. Life is so simple. I am here, happy. There was never any mystery other than me, and there is nothing more to figure out. I am free to do whatever I want. I am free."

After writing, I had the realization that my decision to fully embrace and release life simultaneously, regardless of circumstance, had empowered me in an unexpected way. I felt that I could intend what I wanted of my salvia journey and that outcome would be achieved. With that thought, I got up, went to my wife, and gave her a hug, the trip completed. Looking at the clock, I saw that the peak process had lasted about 40 minutes, much longer than the literature indicates for smoking salvia.

CHAPTER 14

the foundation

A few days later I reported some of my findings to my meditation students, Mark and Donna, who had participated in the introductory salvia session.

After discussing my experiences, both students indicated that they felt pulled to try salvia again, but this time at a higher dosage. Donna had come prepared, having just purchased a salvia package 20 times the strength of a single dosage. I was to be there as the helper, there to ensure safety.

I wondered whether smoking the extra-potency salvia would result in dimensional travel for these students, and whether they would perceive that experience in the same way that I had, i.e., my body digitally unzipping before my perspective was pulled into other people and things. Would they travel through time?

I explained how smoking salvia had initially caused me great fear, but after a few experiences and some important realizations, I became able to move beyond fear through a big change in attitude.

I explained the mindset of simultaneous embrace and surrender to life and all potentialities, even in the face of potential insanity, death, or hell. I explained how giving up my life to love had empowered and purified me, and I recommended that they approach their lives and the plant in this same manner.

Both students agreed that the attitude I had embraced felt right and was a reasonable way to live. They were excited to try this approach with salvia. Both students began meditating themselves into a mindset that accepted all possibilities through love. I asked them to wait until their bodies moved to take the pipe mindlessly.

About ten minutes passed before Mark's hand moved to take the pipe. He took multiple small hits before setting down the pipe. He lay back on the floor. As soon as the pipe was free, Donna filled the bowl and began taking small puffs. After five or six pulls, she began to physically wobble, so I took the pipe from her. As soon as she released the pipe, she collapsed sideways onto the floor from her seated position, her head landing on a pillow.

Within a minute Donna began mumbling

something unintelligible. She would utter one or two words and then stop: "I can't,""This is,""What,""Can you,""What is,""I need,""Help."

Calmly I reminded her that I was with her and to relax. She clumsily kicked out as she tried to rise to her hands and knees in panic. She had almost no balance, so sitting up was an ordeal.

She spoke unintelligibly and crawled toward the far side of the room. Then she said, "I'm,""Can,""You,""Can you,""Help me." I placed my hands on her arm and shoulder to let her know that I was with her. She moved right next to me, seeming to appreciate the support. I lightly hugged her from the side to let her know that I was with her.

"I can't,""What's going,""I'm ...."In a panic she crawled out of the back room and into the larger front room. I was concerned that she was going to try to exit the building. She could not walk, but I was not about to let her out of my sight.

I moved into the larger room and ahead of her to be sure that I could keep her from leaving the building or otherwise hurting herself in any way. No matter what I said, she seemed unable to understand or possibly unable to hear me.

She looked at the front door and then asked intelligibly, "Can you open the door?"

She was beginning to come back, but clearly she was still in panic, judging by her bulging eyes.

"No," I said. "I can't let you out. It's dangerous."

"I won't go out. I just need to look outside."

I opened the front door, and from a distance Donna peered outside.

"Okay, I am going to go back into the room now," she said, as she turned and crawled. I closed the door and followed her back into the room to keep an eye on her. She was still not fully back. Donna calmly lay on her side and rested her head on the pillow, her eyes relaxed. The peak was over.

With that, we began debriefing the experience. Mark said he had not had much of an experience and seemed a bit disappointed. Although he said he felt relaxed and sort of high, he had gone nowhere. I thought that he might be insensitive to salvia, whereas I am probably highly sensitive. I suggested that he consider getting a water bong, which would allow him to take larger puffs comfortably, and I also suggested that he might try a higher potency, if he felt it appropriate.

Donna had fully returned from her trip and sat upright, ready to tell of her experience.

After releasing the pipe, I thought I fell and hit my head hard. Then I was in another place. It was terrifying to be torn away like that so abruptly. I wanted to explain where I was, but just as soon as I began speaking, I was torn away again and in a new place. I don't know why, but I really felt like I needed to explain where I was. I tried to move, but I was torn away and into yet another place. Time was so slow, it was like two frames of time passed, and then I was in still another place. It was so horribly disorienting. I tried to go into this trip with the attitude to accept whatever came through love, but I just couldn't do it. I don't understand how you could

110

transcend the fear. It is just so incredibly overwhelming.

Yes, it is tremendously overwhelming. I had experiences of utter terror before I was able to move beyond the fear. I have smoked salvia multiple times since we last met. In your case, this is your first high-dose trip, so you lacked experience. Lacking experience with the overwhelming power of salvia, it is understandable that you would have an intellectual approach to fear going into the trip. Without sufficient experience, fear is the inevitable result to being ripped away from your life.

Yes, that was exactly the feeling. I was being ripped away from everything that I loved and knew. It was a terrifying feeling. And then there was the fear that I would never get back.

It's like an amateur boxer preparing to have her first pro fight. The coach explains exactly what the experience is going to be like. The young boxer visualizes the match again and again, and she is determined not to be overcome by fear.

Unfortunately, once she's in the ring, she realizes that her opponent, who has some pro experience, is a lot more seasoned than she is, and she begins to wilt under the overwhelming pressure. Fear takes over, and it exhausts her; strategy goes out the window. She loses badly.

The young boxer has lost, and she may be critical of herself. She may feel miserable about her perceived failure, but in reality, she just lacked the experience necessary to even know what getting in the ring with a pro was going to be like. Words are not experience, so no matter how well the coach explained the experience, the young boxer would not understand until she was in there. That is life.

I know you feel a little down about the panic response to salvia, but now you have had your first match, and now you have real experience. You know what your opponent has to offer, and you know where your weaknesses are. Now, you have seen the actuality of salvia. Now you have a foundation for moving through your fear and into unconditioned love. Without going through the experience, there was no way for you to really know what to expect. Now you know how to prepare. The next time you try salvia, should there be another time, you will go into it having digested much of the fear that you experienced tonight, and you will likely make real progress. I am not recommending that you try salvia again. That is completely up to you.

I really didn't like the experience. It was awful, but now I feel more than ever that I need to do it again—not today ... maybe next week. I will try again when the time is right.

What I don't understand is how you could do this without anyone watching over you. I have heard of people running in panic through sliding glass doors or falling into swimming pools. It's dangerous. It is easy to imagine how people can get hurt using salvia. The fear is just so overwhelming. Weren't you concerned that you would have a panic attack and get hurt?

I always do what feels right deep down. For me, in this case, it felt right to do alone. My wife was in the house with me, and she knew what I was doing, and there was nothing in the room that I could hurt myself with, so it really wasn't very dangerous. That said, after much time on the path of awakening, I have discovered that I can trust the pulling feeling, and the feeling was to do salvia alone. Anyway, for me, listening to my body works very well. If I think, then things get out of whack. But I always take responsibility for what comes of "my choices."

We adjourned for the evening and met again the following week. Donna had thought about the experience over the week and had some questions for me.

I am a mother and I feel that I have to be responsible for my children. It seems to me that going into the psychedelic experience with the idea that I might die or go insane is irresponsible. Wouldn't it be better not to take a substance like that? I love my children, and I would not want them to suffer because I made an irresponsible decision.

Have you researched *Salvia divinorum*?

No, I haven't. I just trusted what you told me about it.

113

Blindly trusting me, or anyone for that matter, is irresponsible, isn't it? As you said, you need to be responsible as a mother. The responsible thing in this case would be to research salvia.

I do not want you to blindly trust what I say. The benefit of researching is that you will know that you have taken responsibility, and you will know what you found in your search. You won't be wondering if what I told you was right or not. And if things go badly, you will not have anyone to blame for the outcome.

Regarding the mindset to the salvia experience, I am not saying that you should go into the experience thinking that you may die or go insane. What I am suggesting is that you live your life with happiness, come what may, be it pleasant or unpleasant, embracing and releasing fully in every moment.

It is a way of being that is applied to everything that you do, including a psychedelic, should you feel pulled to take one. If love is only used as a tactic to get through a salvia experience, then that love is not authentic. It is a lie born of fear, is it not?

The love that I speak of is a way of being, not a tactic. It is not born of fear but of inspiration based on the realization that there is no other sane choice but to love. Love, because that is the only thing that makes sense.

The irony is, when you embrace life fully through love while simultaneously releasing your life in every moment, fear no longer has a grip on you. You find that you are free in a way that you could not imagine before living unconditionally.

The power that I speak of is so simple that our logical minds simply overlook it. There is nothing profound about it. It's just so obvious once you see it.

I think I am ready to take salvia again. I totally feel what you are saying, and now I see how fear had distorted my perception of what you were telling me last week. I get it now. You are talking about a way of life, and a way of being that would benefit my life and my children's lives. It is really powerful.

That night Donna went to the other side and came back laughing. She laughed and laughed for about ten minutes before she was ready to talk. She explained that she was transported just as had happened in her previous trip, but this time, it was not scary as it had been before. What had seemed impossible to her just a week earlier now seemed so ridiculously simple. She had faced her fears with love and transcended them. That is the way.

CHAPTER 15

the big picture

During my salvia trips, I saw that everything had awareness and a window of perception into the universe. Even "objects" like molecules, atoms, and subatomic particles feel and suffer from the environments that they are in.

These objects inherit the atmospheres projected by human beings. If a person is genuinely happy, then so is the physical space around that person. On a feeling level your attitude means everything to the space around you.

Although I had received from the salvia experience

the perspective that everything feels, I had received similar understandings from "natural" visions and through many meditation experiences over the span of my life.

I often feel, and sometimes see, the glow of awareness in my surroundings, but *Salvia divinorum* offered me a new perspective into the phenomenon. It allowed me to perceive the world as if I were the object.

A sudden realization came over me. Now that I could direct the salvia experience with my intention, I could use the sage to get a bigger picture of reality to see what practical wisdom might be there.

Two full days went by before I was pulled again to smoke salvia. I waited to see what, if any, prayer or intention would arise before my hand took the pipe. After a few minutes, I knew what was to occur. I was to stop the transport process just in the midst of returning to my body, so that I could get a look at the world of my body, the world of the abyss, and the world that I was moving out of at the same time.

A few minutes later my hand reached for the pipe, and my journey began. I found myself as an atom in the rubber at the bottom of some man's left shoe. Of course, from the perspective of the rubber, I could not see the man; I could only perceive the ground beneath his shoe. I did not remember Richard or my intention to stop in the middle of the transfer. I was just an atom in rubber for a time.

Eventually the wind kicked up and began pulling my perspective out of the rubber, stretching it through the abyss and into the body of Richard. I stopped the transport process there, and I began exploring the three perspectives. From this stretched-out vantage, I could clearly see the human being, whose shoe I was a part of, and the street that he was walking along. I could see the wind attempting to pull me through dimensions, and I could see the room that Richard was in from my physical eyes. I was stretched through a two-dimensional door and seeing two worlds simultaneously. From this perspective, it was clear that the universe that Richard lived in existed within a particle within the atom within the rubber of that man's shoe.

I saw that within a single atom, there exist multiple universes that are filled with uncountable perspectives, as is our universe, perspectives that are no more or less real and meaningful than yours or mine.

Although most of these perspectives wished to be happy, many were not, owing to the atmosphere of their surroundings.

I could look up, into the universe that the man with the shoe was in, and know that his universe was but a "particle" in an atom of a still larger universe, which was located in a "particle" in the atom of one larger still, and so on, forever. The experience was like seeing infinite bubbles that are located inside a larger bubble that is but one of infinite bubbles inside a still larger bubble, which was one of infinite bubbles in yet another larger bubble, and so on, endlessly.

Looking down at my own shoe, I realized that universes get progressively smaller, universe within atom, within universe, within atom, within universe within atom ... forever.

Look at your shoe. How many universes could be there, filled with perspectives much like yours?

No matter where I looked there were individual perspectives, within perspectives, within perspectives. The fullness of my love helped them to be happy. If I was miserable, then the atoms around me, and the universes within me, were also miserable. I felt a sense of responsibility larger than anything I had ever felt in my life. What I think and feel makes a difference, even if I can't always see it.

CHAPTER 16

beyond excuses

After seeing the larger picture during my last trip, it felt right to increase the dosage of the salvia from fivefold potency to three times that strength, in order to look still deeper and further. I took several intentional trips, but no matter from which perspective I looked, the same basic principles applied. My feelings and expression in the world were felt by everything around me, and it made a difference, a big difference.

Then everything became so obvious. The answer was so simple that it was impossible to miss. No matter who, where, or what you are, so long as perception is happening, why not make the best of it? Why be a stinker? Acknowledging that you have or maybe even *are* perception, the only thing that makes any sense is to love, and to love in such a way that buoys everyone and everything around us. There is no need for creepy love. There is no need to grow some long beard, cross your legs, and call yourself a guru.

After taking some time to really think about my experiences with ayahuasca, psilocybin, and *Salvia divinorum*, I was exposed to a lot of utterly amazing concepts that could be described as truths, but I do not believe them, for to do so would be to step out of the nexus point and back into the darkness of a divided mind.

I have realized that my beliefs can do nothing to stop the collapse of society if that is what is coming. I also realized that if Christ/Buddha is real, again my belief is irrelevant, for reality shows up despite beliefs.

I realized that the single most productive thing that I could do to be of use in this world was simply to be happy with no excuses, and to help others to be even happier.

I also realized that whenever I am not happy, that moment is a signpost indicating the things within that are blocking the experience of love. Once I see that sign, the next reasonable step is to work persistently, little by little, to transform what is blocking good cheer, to heal that sickness, for to express anything other than benevolence is sickness.

When we are sick we don't feel well, so quite naturally we will share that misery with the world unconsciously. It's not really a choice, is it? Only when benevolence shines through could that choice even be considered a possibility, and once benevolence is constant, would you ever choose a negative attitude? You wouldn't, would you? So, if you are healthy, is there really a choice?

Maybe we are all just moved along by the forces of the sheer magnitude of the awesome Oneness of which our perception is but one tiny little window. Maybe there is no choice. Maybe the writing of this book, and the reading of it, might not constitute choice—I don't know. If it's not a choice, that's okay, because I can't take credit for writing it, and you can't take credit for reading it. If the force that led to the writing of this book helps you to be a little happier, then I am blessed just to be a part of your happiness, even in a small way.

Then again, maybe there is choice, but in such a case the only choice worth making is the choice of love. If choice is the case, and love makes sense to you, then the only thing left to learn is how to heal the sickness that has been blocking the full expression of love.

I suspect that half of the awakening process is just getting to the point where the body realizes that love is the only game in town worth playing. Maybe the other half of the path is facing up to the fears that keep it from consistently playing that game.

The game of love is both lighthearted and deep, for

a true expression of love overflows your body and floods the people around you with its good cheer. It ripples out to society, to the world, and to the very heart of being—today, tomorrow, forever.

Many powerful tools are available to help you face and transform your fears, and thereby unveil unconditioned love in your life. There is meditation, prayer, dream awareness, autonomic releasing, daily life intention, and maybe, if you feel so pulled, there is the psychedelic. But whatever you choose, go into the process with the utmost respect, for you may find yourself face to face with your most powerful demon or even the source of all that is.

And no matter what you have accomplished, how much you know, how many visions that you have, be aware, none of it trumps the simplest thing—*love*.

CHAPTER 17

the method

The two "trickster" mushroom journeys would probably qualify as "bad trips" for most people. If you feel that way, you might be likely to assume that I would be unwilling to take psilocybin again, but you'd be incorrect. I went into each of these journeys praying to perceive my unseen darkness, so the possibility of going through hell was not lost on me. That said, the first trip was way beyond any suffering that I could possibly have imagined before taking psilocybin.

Going into the second journey, I expected no less than the first. It's not that I wanted to suffer—I'm not masochistic. I simply understand that one must face one's inner demons to really see and undo their fiendish grip on the soul and so become a fully realized human being.

It seems to me that to follow the pathway to inner peace is to consciously enter one's personal hell with love and courage, and in so doing see through the inequity that lies within. For me, embracing suffering is merely about recovering integrity. After all, the stuff that is buried within affects people around us, even if we are unaware of it. Taking responsibility for what lies within means taking a good honest look at it and fully experiencing it through right attitude.

Many people are simply unwilling to dive into their unseen darkness, and that reluctance is completely understandable. After all, if it were easy, everyone would already be doing it. The very reason that we've not done it yet is that we don't want to look at what lies down there. It's painful. It's terrifying. I can't blame anyone for wanting to avoid that stuff. But in my experience, the benefits of diving in are well worth the temporary suffering it entails, no matter how bad that pain and suffering may be.

If one is willing to see one's inner demons, psychedelics are not the only way to do it. We can begin to see our inner demons through certain types of meditation, certain types of energy work, through our dreams, and even through simple intention and curiosity in daily life.

Psychedelics constitute just one of many diving boards—and a high-dive at that. For my personal path, psilocybin was appropriate. It helped to so greatly amplify previously unnoticed darkness and made it impossible to overlook, impossible to avoid. I am thankful for that benefit, and I fully accept the pain that went along with the process. After all, it was my prayer to see that darkness—a prayer that was answered.

From my perspective, the world is a little better off each time someone takes a positive step toward resolving the veil of darkness, regardless of methodology.

If one feels pulled to take psilocybin, be aware that, although very rare, a trickster-motivated death could come from the amplifying power of the mushroom. Although deaths directly attributable to psilocybin overdose are unheard of, in rare cases, individuals have committed suicide while on the substance. Judging from the wood stove incident, it's easy to imagine how those suicides may have occurred against the individuals' will.

Although also rare, the most likely cause of death with psilocybin comes from mixing it with other drugs, especially alcohol. Deaths due to mixing almost always stem from using the substance to party. Psilocybin is a powerful teacher that should never be taken lightly. Respect it as such and you are heading in the right direction. If, for any reason, you are going to take psilocybin, think hard before consuming any other mind-altering substance in conjunction with it.

For safety's sake, if you decide to use psychedelics, carefully remove all possible dangers from your journey location before the ceremony begins. No sharp objects, no guns, no fire-making apparatuses, and no pills. Consider what the trickster might use against you, and then eliminate every such possibility.

Apart from preparing a safe journey space, it is also wise to have someone else nearby who can protect you. Were it not for my wife, I have little doubt that I would have died during my first trip. Having a helper in the same room with you may not work well, though, as the presence of another person nearby may create a sense of self-consciousness that could hold you back and prevent you from really "going there." If you decide to have someone watch over you, be sure that it is someone who is well-read and experienced with the psychedelic at the dosage that you are taking it, because inexperienced people are likely to overreact to the anguish and other strange things that may be going on with you during your trip. Finally, be sure that your helper is someone whom you trust thoroughly.

Mindset and Setting

Mindset and physical setting are both very important because your trip will probably arise from your mental state as well as your surroundings. It might be unwise to consume a high dose of psilocybin in a place with a bad vibe. To stimulate a positive mindset and setting, many people take psilocybin outdoors in natural settings, where they create a large circle surrounded by stones. They sit within that circle, which symbolizes a womb. If you fear the outdoors, then having your ceremony indoors may be the better option. Wherever you are planning to take your trip, adjust it according to your intuition. Only you know what makes you feel at ease. *Note: psilocybin can dilate the pupils and make the eyes light sensitive, so journeying at night or in a somewhat darkened room appeals to many people.*

Be sure to have blankets to warm the body in case your body temperature drops. Also be sure to have fresh, warm, potable water readily available. I use a thermos for my purposes. You might never use these things, but not having them around when you need them could prove regrettable.

The main difference between the approach that I personally use and the one that is usually recommended is, in a nutshell, that I am not trying to avoid "bad trips." In fact, I found those trips to be extraordinarily beneficial. When I hear someone describe a trip as being bad, it tells me more about the individual's default attitude than it does about the trip, which may have carried a profound lesson that was entirely lost on the individual because of mindset.

If you want to see your inner demons, and move beyond them, then go into the ceremony respectfully and take the time to feel your way through the preparation, which includes securing the proper setting, asking others for assistance, and preparing the mushrooms as is appropriate for you. Feel your way through any questions that you may have and any prayers that you may feel drawn to utter. If all preparation is right, then it is also likely that you have the correct mindset.

With regard to mindset, the key point is to approach the experience with love and with the determination to learn from whatever happens. As you may be intending to enter into your personal hell, it is possible that the experience will be unpleasant.

The desire to avoid the unpleasant may mean that you are not sincere about resolving those issues. Such a desire is born of fear. The irony is that fear is usually the energy that feeds those demons. Love and courage lead to transformation, regardless of the path. Go with those powers to the extent that you can. The more that you employ love and courage in the face of fear, the easier it will be to do so the next time around.

Consider that psilocybin is merely unlocking information that does not normally make its way into your window of perception. If you take responsibility for what is held within, then there is no such thing as a bad trip. A single four-hour dive, depending on attitude, can benefit your entire life thereafter. That's a miraculous return on investment. How is that bad?

What you will discover by intentionally choosing to see your inner demons is that you are ever more capable of facing them with each experience, which is an extraordinarily empowering realization once you have it. Not only do you feel more capable and empowered, but your life experience also improves, and that benefit also spills over to the people around you.

At this stage you have taken responsibility and authority in your life. You are no longer a reactive victim. And that is powerfully inspiring. Discovering the right attitude is the key to awakening and to life.

Conversely, if you accidentally happen upon your inner hell and you shrink from it, you may fall ever deeper into the sandtraps of victimization and fear. Each time that you shrink from your responsibility, you are further diminished. You may physically survive, but what sort of life is that?

To take authority in your life, simply choose to face your issues, to really see them, to really feel them without defending them, without identifying with them, to move through and beyond them with love.

Simply making this choice gives you the power to do exactly that. You can start small and work on to ever larger challenges, little by little, as you move through life. And with each resultant success, you will thereby gain more confidence in your ability to move through negativity and into a more positive way of being. That said, there is no need to grab Satan's tail on your first dive. You can start out small and work your way up to larger and larger challenges progressively. And you don't necessarily need psychedelics to embrace this approach, for it is a way of life.

If you do go the route of psychedelics, typically the psychedelic will sort out your challenge for you. You get what you get. I do not recommend fighting the process. If you've taken sufficient potency to bring you to hell, you are not going to be able to stop the process anyway; after all, the substance is in your body. After a few hours the trip will wind down, though during the trip you may feel that it will never end.

Instead of resisting, accept that you might die. Accept that you might go insane, and in spite of those possibilities, be determined to learn. Based on the safety profile for psilocybin, chances are extremely high that you will survive and be a stronger person for it. Again, during the trip you might not believe the substance's safety statistics.

Q & A

Is the trickster that you describe in your visions a character from folklore?

I chose the word "trickster" as a description of the entity. I do not associate that entity with folklore characters, although the character in my visions may represent an archetype.

If I take ayahuasca, psilocybin mushrooms, or Salvia divinorum, *can I expect to have the same realizations that you had?*

If I set aside the specific story of each trip and instead look at the effects that the trips had on me psychologically, I would liken the psychedelic experiences that I had to a press that squeezed my mind so tightly as to cause my disharmonies to rise up, into the window of conscious perception.

It seems to me that these substances are part of an equation that is largely made up of your own mind. Everything that you carry with you into the psychedelic trip is grist for the mill. Everything that you have studied, the wisdom that you have acquired, the degree of psychological integration and sensitivity that you have achieved all make a difference. The mindset of the moment and the momentum of your life fuel the experience on psychedelics, just as does every other aspect of your life experience.

The main difference between your daily life experience and the experience of psychedelics—with the method that I employ, at least—is that with psychedelics, what you hold within is intensely amplified and packed into a compressed time-frame. Imagine the emotional content of a lifetime being amplified 100 times and crushed into the space of a few hours.

I suspect individuals lacking the motivation to awaken will get nothing like what I got out of the experience. If you don't want to or are unready to see your inner darkness, then to you, an inner hell experience may simply be a considered a "bad trip." If you are not on the awakening path, then even if the trip is pleasant, to you it may be just another form of entertainment.

I ate psilocybin mushrooms regularly growing up. They grew like weeds in my area, so instead of smoking pot, we kids just ate mushrooms. I never really got any guidance from the experience, so I'm not sure that taking mushrooms could provide any real benefits to my life now.

Were you a "know-it-all" teenager at that time?

Yes. We all were.

Intention seems to play a large role in the experience, maybe the largest role. As you were coming into the experience in a psychologically closed manner, uninterested in learning or introspection, it is unlikely that you would get much of a lesson from psilocybin or any other psychedelic. As you are interested in awakening now, you would be entering into the psychedelic experience with a completely different mindset than when you were a teenager. Thus, it is likely that you would have a very different experience this time around.

But in your journeys you were often scolded for your arrogance. Why wasn't I scolded in the same manner when I was a teenager?

Bear in mind that I went into the psychedelic experience, wishing to learn and to have my darkness magnified so that it could be seen and healed. I was interested in seeing the root of my remaining disharmony. I wanted that disharmony to be amplified. Fundamentally, I was not comparing my disharmony to that of other people. Instead, I was comparing it to harmony. Compared to harmony, even a little disharmony is a noisy thing.

I suspect that if I were entering the psychedelic experience with a closed attitude, the experiences would have been entirely different.

Do you think psychedelics would help anyone who is interested in spirituality?

The word "spirituality" is so broad in meaning as to be nearly meaningless in communication unless some consensus on its meaning is isolated by the individuals. The search for truth is commonly considered to be a spiritual pursuit. But the mind can never understand truth, so whatever it is that the mind apprehends in the search for truth almost inevitably becomes another belief, another idol—a maze of ego. While the connected nature of the universe can be experienced, it can't be understood. The attempt to understand it comes from the desire to control it, the trickster.

Feel into these two intentional prayers to see the differences between them. "Show me the ultimate truth," and "Show me my remaining disharmony."

The first prayer comes from the desire to understand truth, to mentally encapsulate it and control it. The very intention is born of the assumption that there is an ultimate truth—an ego projection.

The second prayer is dedicated to inner correction, something that potentially benefits you, everyone around you, and *all that is*—a prayer that is born of the experiential awareness that something harmonious lies at the very core of being.

Both prayers could be called spiritual, due to the vagueness of the word, but, to the nervous system, the two prayers are universes apart. The first is based in assumption, while the second is based in experiential awareness and feeling.

Both prayers may lead to suffering, but the first prayer leads to long-term suffering because it binds the soul, while the second prayer leads one through temporary suffering as it frees the soul.

The intention to see the truth leads to long-term suffering because the truth revealed then becomes a belief system that leads into the maze of ego, where the truth then serves as the judge of self, others, and society, causing untold suffering.

The prayer to see one's inner disharmony may also lead to intense temporary suffering as bound-up energy may need to be fully experienced before it can be fully digested. Once the individual fully experiences the bound energy through intention, the bound energy transforms to reveal an underlying experience of harmony that the mind cannot grasp, and in so doing the suffering of that bound energy ceases.

The differences between the two prayers may seem subtle, but they are born of two very different mindsets—one that seeks to control, and the other that seeks to flow.

I think psychedelic visions are just hallucinations. I want to awaken naturally and of my own efforts.

I cannot address whether you should or should not take psychedelics, for that is entirely up to you. Instead, I would like to address the assumption that human beings can do anything "on their own."

Human beings are, by nature, interdependent creatures. You are integrally connected to your environment and the people around you. You can't get through a single day without outside inputs. You need food, water, and information from other people. If you are on the awakening path, you have surely learned from many teachers either directly or indirectly. Do you get credit for that information?

What is the difference between a teaching from a person and one from a psychedelic? The main difference that I see is that with people, you can easily avoid, ignore, argue, or run away, whereas with psychedelics, you're stuck until the trip is over, and being stuck can have its benefits.

When I hear someone say, "I want to awaken naturally on my own," I wonder if those words are born of a form of arrogance or pride. For what does it mean to do it on your own? What does it mean to do it naturally? *Natural* is a word that is nearly meaningless in a universe that is entirely natural.

If I could summarize what it was that the psychedelic experience did for me, it would be to show me perspectives that I had never considered. If ten people were shown those very same perspectives, would they all come to the same conclusion? I doubt it. The work that I did coming into the experience helped me to discover a simple wisdom behind the perspectives that I was offered.

Prior to the psilocybin and salvia trips, I spent a lot of time testing attitudes and ways of being in daily life to see what was functional. Surely, all of that work was included in the trips. Do I get credit or does the plant get credit? Does it matter? And if it does matter, to whom does it matter? If you say "It matters to me," is not that feeling born of the very thing that creates the sense of separation and suffering, the ego, which you are trying to transcend?

In the end, it is up to each individual to do what

feels right. I would just caution the motivation that may be hiding in words like "I want to do it on my own," for those words carry the odor of the trickster.

I like the way that my brain works. I am afraid that taking any psychedelic will permanently alter my brain in some way.

There is evidence that psychedelics permanently alter the brain, similar to how long-term meditation alters the brain. If you are happy with how your brain works and have no desire for the changes attributed to psychedelic use or meditation, I can see no reason you would want to take psychedelics or meditate. For more information on psychedelics and the brain, see the Appendix.

I have a friend who suffers from psychotic episodes from time to time. Do you think psychedelics could help him?

I am not a doctor, and so I cannot give any medical advice. Furthermore, there is insufficient scientific information to ground my opinions, but I am happy to share my general outlook on this topic.

It is speculated that the Vikings used psychedelics before going on their raids. It appears that they may have used *Amanita muscaria* (fly agaric), which contains a psychoactive compound called muscimol—a psychedelic very different from psilocybin—before invading and slaughtering people. As their intention was malicious, the psychedelic may have amplified that malicious intent. Charles Manson and his followers, known as the Manson Family, claim to have used LSD and psilocybin in their regular rituals.

The Manson Family's murderous spree, and the societal level of fear that it created, may well have been a factor in the reactive banning of psychedelics in the 1970s. Manson was psychotically deranged. Did psilocybin play a role in those murders? I don't know, but maybe.

I actually knew a person who exchanged letters with Charles Manson, while Manson was in prison. I read one of Manson's letters, and it was deeply, deeply disturbing. That man was deranged beyond my capacity to articulate. He signed his letter in his own blood. Apparently psilocybin and LSD didn't help him much, because it's hard to imagine anyone being more deranged than Manson. Maybe psychedelics made things worse in his case. In my opinion, a lot more research needs to be done on these substances and their interaction with such mental illnesses as psychosis.

I approached psychedelics with the intention to bring out, or magnify, what was within me to improve my health and to better society. I apply the same mindset to all life experience and find it to be highly beneficial.

Until there is solid research that says otherwise, individuals with a personal or family history of mental illness might be better off staying far away from psychedelics, for the sake of the individual and society. I would suggest that your friend consult his mental health provider before taking any mind-altering substances.

I've had some amazing journeys on psychedelics, and I have been shown incredible truths, just as you have, but you seem to be somewhat skeptical of what you were shown. Why?

Even if an unimaginably powerful presence came to me, claiming to be God, and, for some reason, I believed the claim, I would not kill even if I were ordered to do so by that God. Whatever I do or do not do is guided by what feels right to me. To behave otherwise would turn me into a victim of life. Surely there is some degree of malevolence, delusion, and deceit in everyone. We should not assume that everything we receive through a vision comes from a pure place of benevolence. Question everything, and take responsibility. Consider everything to be theory until you can determine what is functional. That is the only way to remain in balance.

Isn't taking a skeptical approach to the visions that one receives during psychedelic trips tantamount to resisting those visions? I have heard that resisting psychedelic visions is unhealthy.

Personally, when I receive advice that I am unsure about, no matter the source, initially I just listen to them, without agreement or disagreement. If I can ask questions, I ask. Over time the advice simmers within, in some cases for many years, before insight is reached on that advice.

Even when I have found what appears to be conclusive evidence that disproves the advice, I do not entirely throw away the advice, because I have discovered through my awakening process that sometimes my initial perspective is faulty because it is based on a crude awareness. As awakening progresses, we get a progressively broader and higher-resolution view of things, and that clearer perspective serves as a correcting mechanism.

As advice is processed over time, I allow questions to arise, and then I see where those questions take me. It is an exploration that sometimes leads to unexpected gold.

So do you accept all advice equally, regardless of the source? That would seem foolish and dangerous. After all, should I accept equally the health advice of my beerbuddy and my doctor?

No, of course not. I give a more weight to an expert than to a layman, but even with "an expert," I reserve some space for skepticism. I keep at least half an ear open with anyone. Sometimes, although rarely, the fool has something smart to add to the conversation.

With regard to visions, I have found there to be lies. Consider how the trickster told me that my wife did not love me. Clearly that was not a true statement.

Personally, I do not resist a vision in process. Instead, I relax as much as possible and simply allow the vision to take its course. If I can ask questions in the vision, I do so. If I can't ask during the vision, I am sure to ask my inner space after the vision.

Regardless of the source of information, I take responsibility for what I do and do not accept. Taking responsibility is part of taking authority in your life. To do otherwise is to take a passive approach that leads to weakness, insecurity, irresponsibility, and feelings of victimization. Those feelings eventually result in hopelessness, resentment, and nihilism—powerful demons indeed.

The psychedelic substances that you took all seem to have great safety profiles. From my research, they don't seem to be dangerous, so why are you so cautious with them?

Anyone could have an allergy to any substance. You never know for sure until you take a substance, do you? For that reason, I do not make recommendations other than to exercise a reasonable degree of caution whenever consuming anything new. But beyond the possibility of adverse allergic reaction, I always recommend caution when approaching a powerful teacher, psychedelic or otherwise. I feel that a healthy portion of respect is warranted when approaching any teacher, for you may not get exactly what you expect.

Will taking psychedelics solve my problems?

Even if you feel pulled to take these substances, it is not a good idea, in my opinion, to assume that the psychedelic is going resolve your life problems. You need to be invested in yourself and work little by little, daily, to make lasting improvements.

The ayahuasca experience that I describe in Chapter 1 was extremely powerful and interesting, but I would not have distilled any real value out of it had I not worked to verify the teachings received through that vision. The vision served as guidance, but my feet need to do the walking to see if the guidance leads anywhere of value.

My brother is clearly depressed. He considers himself to be on the awakening path. Would it be a good idea for him to try psychedelics with your method?

I can't give such advice, but early studies on psilocybin indicate some promise regarding depression. The visions that result from taking psilocybin appear to help people make lasting beneficial changes in their lives. From preliminary studies it would seem that a plant intervention can help people to get a fresh perspective and thereby break a negative cycle.

Some people can get in such depressed and/or anxious states that they simply can't or won't do anything productive. I am hopeful that more studies will be conducted on psychedelics and their capacity to help people to break out of depression, anxiety, and addiction. The preliminary evidence is quite positive. I discuss these studies in the Appendix.

I know a person who uses ayahuasca every weekend. I have known her for years, and I have not seen any substantial positive changes in her life. I think psychedelics are a crutch.

Yes, I too have met such individuals. Psychedelics, like anything, can be misused. Some people seem to rely on psychedelics to have a spiritual feeling. Information comes easily, but they do nothing with it. Without taking the time to verify and incorporate the lessons learned, it seems to me that psychedelics can become just another form of escape from reality. A week between ceremonies seems to be way too short a period to verify and incorporate what could be received from a mystical experience.

People who use psychedelics or any substance to get a spiritual feeling may be unaware that spirituality is not a choice. Everyone is equally spiritual. There is nothing that you could ever do to make yourself any more or less a part of all that is than you already are.

144

If for some reason we are blocked from daily awareness of connection to all that is, then taking psychotropics can be an easy way to get that spiritual feeling. The downside is, we may feel that we need psychotropics to have that spiritual feeling.

Whatever your spiritual practices, if your motivations and intentions are clear and sincere, then you will probably learn something valuable from those practices.

If you wish to have a sense of connectedness in your daily life, you will need to incorporate spiritual practices into your daily life. Taking psychedelics on a daily basis would be ill-advised, but what we learn from the perspectives offered through psychedelic experiences could potentially be put into daily practice.

How do I know if it is right for me to take psychedelics?

The answer is both obvious and complicated. In my case, the pull was undeniable.

What do you mean when you say "the pull"?

When I say "pull," I do not mean desire. In many cases the pull has led me to do things that I really did not want to do. Always the pull has led me to do what was in the best interest of spiritual awakening.

It is important not to confuse the pull with urge,

compulsion, or desire. The feeling of the pull comes from a much deeper place within than do any of those other forces. The pull is not rational and should not be justified. If the motivation for doing something is a narrative in your mind—for example, "I'll make more money if I take this job"—that is not what I mean by *the pull*. If you remove all reasons and there is still a pull, then ask deeply within yourself, "Do I just need to do this for the best good of all involved?" If the answer is "Yes," then you have your answer.

What if I don't get an answer?

Then ask the question and follow it by slowly answering both "yes" and "no," with a good pause between each to feel the answers. Feel which answer feels deep and which one feels shallow. The one that feels deeper or wider will be your answer. The one that is shallow and hollow is incorrect. Practicing feeling words brings about heightened awareness of "the pull."

What if they feel the same?

Then there may be no pull, or you've yet to develop sufficient awareness to feel the pull. If you intellectualize this process you will block the source of the pull, which is found in the autonomic nervous system. You have to be able to feel into the process to make progress. People who have been practicing this sort of feeling over time will be more able to get accurate guidance with this method than those who have not.

"The pull" sounds like some sort of psychic phenomenon.

I am not talking about anything psychic here, but simply a form of inner guidance that comes from the nervous system. Your body has ways of communicating that are not logical or emotional, and a person who has relied too much on rationality or emotion may miss some of these messages.

Are you saying that thinking and emotion are wrong?

No, not at all. Thinking and emotion are just two of many tools available to the human being. You need more than a hammer and a nail to build a house. You need other tools beyond rationality, will power, and emotion to walk the path of awakening.

I feel like my inner compass is broken, and I just don't trust myself. What can I do then?

There are several reasons the inner compass can spin out of control. First is that your body does not trust the guidance of the ego, which means that your body is rebelling.

Rebellion can result from being overly willful and domineering over your body. It is helpful to imagine that your body is not you, but is instead more like your lifelong pet. The body has its own direction and proclivities. You can't just order it around all the time and expect that it will obey.

The ego and the body need to form an alliance. This alliance is formed through good leadership. If you are interested in meditation, you will find great information on inner leadership in my book *Inspirience: Meditation Unbound.*

Other reasons that the inner compass can be amiss are energy bound in conscience, false inner narratives, and or traumas, which effectively block awareness of the deep, clear inner space where inner guidance can be found. These topics are also discussed in *Inspirience: Meditation Unbound.*

As a result of bound energy, the body may be in a perpetual survival mode, and so you may need to explore and release the inner sources of bound energy or traumas before you can get clear answers.

No matter what you do, if you are going develop trust with the body, then you will need to follow through on your words and listen to your body. Trust can't be faked, and it doesn't develop overnight.

Can't psychedelics help me to clarify my inner compass?

Psychedelics can provide a fresh perspective and help

to resolve bound energy and trauma to bring more inner clarity. The resulting clarity may unbind the inner compass.

Yes, but if my compass is off before taking psychedelics, how do I know if I should be taking psychedelics?

Absent the inner pull, how have you made any decision in your life?

I just do whatever I want to do or what I am obligated to do.

How has that worked so far?

I'm not where I want to be in life.

If desire and obligation are all that you have to work with right now, and if you are unwilling to develop an alliance with your body, then, practically speaking, desire and willpower may be the only forces available to you. Do you want to try psychedelics? And do you feel that such action will benefit you and those around you?

Yes, I am very tempted. I think they may help me, and if I am in a better place for taking psychedelics, then that would be good for those around me as well.

If you decide to take psychedelics, carefully research, choose your psychedelic well, consider safety, then take responsibility for your choice.

In your journeys, it seems that you developed a power to precisely control what you were going to experience and work on during the trip. My trips seem to be completely random, which is to say that I have no idea what I will get out of them ahead of time, and during the trip I am effectively powerless. In your case, you were easily able to stop where you wanted to stop and explore what you wanted to explore.

Powerful shamans are able to work, through intention, with psychedelics in very specific ways to achieve desired outcomes. What you will find is that the more you practice intention by feeling into your inner hell, with or without psychedelics, the more refined will be your intention and awareness.

Once you have realized a sufficient degree of psychological integration born of awareness and intention, "your" intentions will not feel egoic in the least. Instead, intentions will arise of their own accord, absent the feeling of "you."

When you reach the point of inner harmony and oneness of body and ego, where there is love regardless of outcome, then there will be lucidity during the psychedelic trip. You will be able to effortlessly stop and explore whatever inner guidance leads you to explore. The motivations will not be selfish if you have realized the integrated harmony that I referred to above.

Before I reached sufficient integration, no matter how much willpower I exerted within the psychedelic trip, I was helpless. Once sufficient integration was realized, the power of integration showed up in my life, just as it did in the psychedelic trips, which is to say that daily life is highly empowered, productive, and fulfilling.

As Lao-Tzu states in *Tao Te Ching*, "The greatest wisdom seems childish." Among the many great sages of the past who have shared simple, profound wisdom with the world, we have an 11-year-old child, Ethan, to thank. Be happy—no excuses.

Many Blessings,
Richard L. Haight

If you feel pulled to leave a review for The Psychedelic Path that would be wonderful. You can do so on my Amazon book page. Thank you!

You are also invited to a bonus 13-part audio series "Taking Spiritual Authority in Daily Life" by Richard L. Haight. If you are interested in awakening, you will love it.

www.richardhaight.net

Appendix

Ayahuasca is a traditional Amazonian brew made by combining the ground bark of *Banisteriopsis caapi* with DMT-containing leaves. Traditionally ayahuasca is used by tribes of the Amazon basin for learning, healing, and spiritual ceremony.

Although the ingredients included in the brew can vary somewhat from tribe to tribe, the vine *Banisteriopsis caapi* is a common element. Because DMT, the main psychoactive molecule, is broken down by the stomach's digestive processes, the bark of the *B. caapi* vine, which contains beta-carbolines, is used as a monoamine oxidase inhibitor (MAOI) to prevent the stomach from breaking down DMT, thus allowing the substance to enter the bloodstream and ultimately bind with serotonin receptor sites and facilitate a visionary or mystical experience.

The leaves of *Psychotria viridis* (chacruna), *Diplopterys cabrerana* (chaliponga), or *Psychotria carthagenensis* (amyruca) are variously used for their known psychoactive compound, dimethyltryptamine (DMT).

152

Although ayahuasca is a term that traditionally references these Amazonian brews, the term has been generalized in modern culture to refer to any brew that contains DMT and beta-carbolines, regardless of the source or tradition.

In nontraditional brews, a number of plants can be used to fulfill the DMT/beta-carboline requirement, with the most common sources for beta-carbolines being Syrian rue or *Peganum harmala*. DMT is typically extracted from *Mimosa hostilis* (maiden's wattle) in northern latitudes and *Acacia maidenii* (jurema) in Australia. Although these organisms are the most common sources for such compounds, both DMT and beta-carbolines are fairly common compounds found in a number of plants and trees around the world.

Effects

Shamans commonly refer to ayahuasca as a teacher because they often encounter the "spirit of ayahuasca," by whom they are instructed. Revelations about one's own life and about the universe are common. Often, ayahuasca experience provides guidance to individuals and helps them clean up their lives. People often describe having a spiritual awakening after taking ayahuasca, and some describe gaining access to higher dimensions and spiritual realms.

The most common physical aftereffect of

ayahuasca is purging, which can include vomiting, diarrhea, and occasionally hot and cold flashes.

The most common adverse mental effect of ayahuasca ingestion is profound but temporary emotional distress.

Although long-term negative aftereffects of occasional ayahuasca ingestion have not been sufficiently investigated, there have been reports of symptoms of serotonin syndrome in people who use ayahuasca extensively. Serotonin syndrome symptoms include tremors, diarrhea, autonomic instability, hyperthermia, sweating, muscle spasms, and potentially death.

Legality

Although plants containing DMT are legal to possess, under the International Convention on Psychotropic Substances, DMT is a Schedule I drug. Because of the nature of ayahuasca not lending itself well to partying, thanks to the common purging effect, arrests for DMT are not common when compared to street drugs such as cocaine or marijuana. Even so, the punishments for being caught with DMT can be just as severe as one might receive for possessing or using any illegal street drug, including potential prison time. That stated, certain religious groups that traditionally incorporate psychedelics into religious ceremonies have sued and been granted legal exception. Most notable among these groups are

Santo Daime (ayahuasca) and the Native American Church (peyote).

Safety Profile

Although very rare, deaths linked to ayahuasca consumption have been reported. Most involved use of ayahuasca alongside other psychoactive substances, such as alcohol, recreational drugs, caffeine, nicotine, or antidepressants. Taking ayahuasca while in a physically or mentally compromised state is also not advised.

To date, no LD-50 safety ratings (the dose required to kill 50 percent of rats that receive a specific dosage) for ayahuasca have been completed because ayahuasca is a blanket term that covers many possible plant and compound admixtures.

Research Studies

Assessing the Psychedelic "After-Glow" in Ayahuasca Users: Post-Acute Neurometabolic and Functional Connectivity Changes Are Associated with Enhanced Mindfulness Capacities

The Beckley/Sant Pau Programme published this study in the *International Journal of Neuropsychopharmacology* in 2017. It states that "ayahuasca potentiates mindfulness capacities in volunteers and induces rapid and sustained antidepressant effects in treatment-resistant patients." The study attributes these effects to structural and neural changes in areas of the brain associated with selfhood, ego, and self-control, as well as reward anticipation, decision-making, impulse control, and emotion.

It would appear that ayahuasca creates a situation very similar to that of an advanced meditator with regard to these areas of the brain.

Exploring the Therapeutic Potential of Ayahuasca: Acute Intake Increases Mindfulness-related Capacities

Another study by the Beckley/Sant Pau Programme, published in *Psychopharmacology* in 2016, concluded that "The present findings support the claim that ayahuasca has therapeutic potential and suggest that this potential is due to an increase in mindfulness capacities."

The Alkaloids of Banisteriopsis caapi, the Plant Source of the Amazonian Hallucinogen Ayahuasca, Stimulate Adult Neurogenesis in Vitro

The Beckley/Sant Pau Programme also published a study in 2017 in *Scientific Reports* that finds that "harmine, tetrahydroharmine, and harmaline, the three main alkaloids present in *B. caapi*, and the harmine metabolite harmol, stimulate adult neurogenesis in vitro." *B. caapi* is the main ingredient in traditional Amazonian ayahuasca brews.

The study goes on to state that "These findings suggest that modulation of brain plasticity could be a major contribution to the antidepressant effects of ayahuasca. They also expand the potential application of *B. caapi* alkaloids to other brain disorders...."

Ayahuasca may help your brain to grow neurons, as *B. caapi* "stimulated neural stem cell proliferation, migration, and differentiation into adult neurons." Neurogenesis, the brain's capacity to regrow neurons, could help to mitigate damage from stress, and to stave off depression, schizophrenia, Alzheimer's, and Parkinson's disease.

Of course, these findings may not apply to nontraditional ayahuasca brews, as this study focused specifically on the vine *B. caapi*.

Method of Consumption

Ayahuasca is a brew typically consumed in group ceremonies. Because of the ingredients, the complexity of the brews, and the skills required to make them, ayahuasca is not an easily accessible psychedelic.

Individuals wishing to partake in an ayahuasca ceremony sometimes travel to South America or join a church such as Santo Daime—contexts in which the consumption is legal and the ceremony is led by a skilled practitioner or shaman.

Warning: Because of a burgeoning interest in

ayahuasca ceremonies, some unskilled individuals claiming to be trained shamans are leading ayahuasca ceremonies for profit. Such a situation could be extremely dangerous.

PSILOCYBIN

Psilocybin is a chemical commonly found in the fruiting bodies of certain psilocybe and panaeolus mushrooms. Psilocybin-containing mushrooms commonly occur in human habitats (including such places as lawns, gardens, and road medians) worldwide. Although some species of these mushrooms can be found in more natural settings, they are much easier to find in your garden. The most commonly used psilocybe is Psilocybe cubensis, which grows easily and has an easy-to-detect bluing reaction when damaged, indicating the psychoactive substance.

The common or traditional dose recommendations are based on Psilocybe cubensis. As some psilocybes, such as Psilocybe azurensis, are much more potent than P. cubensis, it is wise to know which genus of psilocybe you are planning to take before determining your dosage. It is also important to note that, even among P. cubensis specimens, the percentage of psilocybin can vary tremendously from mushroom to mushroom. For this reason, you can never truly be sure of your exact psilocybin consumption by ingesting mushrooms. Fortunately, the LD-50 (the amount required to kill 50 percent of the rats given the dosage) of psilocybin is so high that you would have to take 1,000 times the psychoactive dosage, for your body weight, even to potentially kill yourself.

Although there are other known genera of mushrooms that contain psychoactive levels of psilocybin, those species are far less common and are sometimes quite difficult to identify.

Certain conocybes, such as Conocybe cyanopus, do contain psilocybin, but they are dangerous choices because they are quite difficult to identify and they have plenty of deadly look-alikes, so they are generally not used for psychedelic journeys.

Genus gymnopilus is a larger mushroom that has a few psychoactive species, but again, identification can be challenging, and the psilocybin content is often much less, in active species, than you would find in the more easily accessible psilocybes.

Mushroom identification is complicated business, and unless you are highly confident in your mushroom identification skills, and can see color well, you are well advised to avoid harvesting wild mushrooms. As I am color-blind, I am unable to see the tell-tale bluing reaction or spore color of psilocybin mushrooms, so I am ill-suited for mushroom identification.

Note: Just because a mushroom is blue does not mean that it contains psilocybin. What we are looking for with psilocybin mushrooms is a bluing reaction to bruising. That said, not all psychoactive mushrooms bruise blue.

If you are interested in learning more about psychoactive mushrooms and how to identify them, Paul Stamets' book *Psilocybin Mushrooms of the World* is an excellent resource.

Effects

The effects of consuming mushrooms orally can begin anywhere from 20 minutes to two hours after consumption. Typically, such effects last three to six hours. More sensitive people will probably feel the effects sooner than other users, and for some individuals the effects may be many times stronger than would be typical of the average consumer. Still other individuals may feel no effects, even with high doses.

CESAR (Center for Substance Abuse Research) reports that the physical effects of psilocybin use include nausea, vomiting, abdominal cramps, diarrhea, muscle relaxation, weakness, twitches, yawning, drowsiness, dizziness, lightheadedness, lack of coordination, pupil dilation, watering eyes, dry mouth, and facial flushing. Increased heart rate, as well as increased blood pressure and body temperature, are also commonly reported. Other effects include sweating, chills, and shivering, as well as numbness of tongue, lips, or mouth.

CESAR lists the psychological effects from

psilocybin use as heightened sensory experiences, including brighter colors, sharper visual definition, improved hearing acuity, and a more refined sense of taste. One may have auditory, tactile, and visual hallucinations, as well as experiencing synesthesia, which is a melding of the senses, so that one may see music, taste sounds, or hear colors.

Judgment may be impaired, and one may find oneself preoccupied with trivial thoughts, experiences, or objects, as well as having difficulty focusing and maintaining attention.

Other psychological effects include a sense of detachment from one's body that could result in the sense that one has melded with the surroundings. Time and space may be perceptually altered, and visions may be indistinguishable from reality.

Finally, and most importantly for people on the spiritual path, people commonly report having intense mystical experiences of universal oneness and love.

CESAR lists the negative psychological effects as anxiety, restlessness, confusion, disorientation, paranoia, agitation, depression, frightening hallucinations, panic, and terror.

CESAR states that psilocybin is nonaddictive, but a temporary tolerance can build with repeated usage that effectively blocks subsequent trips, even with other hallucinogens such as LSD and mescaline. This tolerance is relatively short lived, with the individual returning to baseline after abstaining for a week.

Looking at the list of possible effects, it would be very easy to classify my experiences with psilocybin as "bad trips," but honestly I found the process to be incredibly beneficial despite the hardship.

Safety Profile

According to CESAR, psilocybin is rated as being more than one-and-a-half times safer than caffeine, three times safer than aspirin, and 30 times safer than nicotine. According to studies on rats, one would need to take 1,000 times more than the effective dose of 6 milligrams (about 1.7 kilograms of dried mushrooms for a 60-kilogram/130-pound person) in order to be fatal.

Legal Status

As safe and psychologically beneficial as psilocybin may be, if you are caught with the substance, you could be charged with a felony, making prison time and all that it entails the single most obvious danger of using psilocybin.

Psilocybin and psilocin are currently listed as Schedule 1 substances by the United States Drug Enforcement Agency's Controlled Substance Act of 1970. The Convention on Psychotropic Substances lists "psilocine, psilotsin" and "psilocybine" as Schedule I substances internationally.

The DEA describes the criteria for listing a

Schedule I substance as follows:

- The drug or other substance has a high potential for abuse
- The drug or other substance has no currently accepted medical use in treatment in the United States
- There is a lack of accepted safety guidelines for use of the drug or other substance under medical supervision

The irony of placing a largely unresearched substance in Schedule I is that it then allows the government to ban or create excessively prohibitive barriers to the process of conducting scientific research into that substance, which deters scientists and medical professionals from making determinations as to the safety, abuse potential, and possible medical benefits of the substance.

Much more research needs to be conducted to properly categorize psilocybin and other similar psychedelics.

Fortunately, in the last decade, there have been several preliminary studies that suggest psilocybin may have profound mental health benefits without any lasting aftereffects.

Research Studies

Psilocybin Can Occasion Mystical-type Experiences Having Substantial and Sustained Personal Meaning and Spiritual Significance

In 2006 a study by Griffiths et al., conducted at Johns Hopkins School of Medicine and published in the *Journal of Psychopharmacology*, shed some light on the potential mental health benefits of having a psilocybin-induced mystical experience.

A psychoactive dose of psilocybin was administered to 36 volunteers, all of whom had no previous psychedelic experience. In the experiment, psilocybin and Ritalin (given as a control and psychedelic placebo) were administered in separate sessions.

After going through these sessions, the volunteers filled out a questionnaire to assess the degree of mystical experience that they had. According to the survey, 61 percent of subjects reported having a "complete mystical experience" after receiving the psilocybin, as compared to 13 percent who reported having a mystical experience after receiving the placebo (Ritalin).

During a follow-up survey two months later, 79 percent of the volunteers reported moderately to greatly increased life satisfaction and a sense of improved well-being. Even though 36 percent of participants reported experiencing "a bad trip" during their psilocybin session, no lasting negative effects were reported by those individuals.

Psilocybin Produces Substantial and Sustained Decreases in Depression and Anxiety in Patients with Life-threatening Cancer: A Randomized Double-blind Trial

In 2016 Roland R. Griffiths et al. published a study in the *Journal of Pharmacology* on the effects of psilocybin in cancer patients suffering from symptoms of depression and/or anxiety.

This trial compared a low dose of psilocybin as a placebo to a high dose administered five weeks later, which was then followed up six months later through patient reports. The high doses produced large decreases in anxiety and depression, and they also improved moods and attitudes in more than 80 percent of the patients, according to the clinician and patient reports. The patients also reported increased optimism, quality of life, and meaning of life. At the six-month follow-up, 80 percent of patients continued to show the decrease in depression and anxiety, as well as increased well-being and life satisfaction.

A detail that intrigued me noted that the benefits reported were dependent upon having a mystical experience. For patients who did not report a mystical experience, the benefits of taking psilocybin were not reported. There were no reports of lasting harm.

Methods of Use

Fresh or dried psilocybin mushrooms can be ingested orally. Dried mushrooms can be ground into powder and then put into capsules to be washed down with water or other liquid to help avoid the unpleasant taste of the mushroom.

For determining dosages, dried *P. cubensis* is generally considered to be the standard. The threshold for the minimum psychoactive dose is a quarter of a gram, so a low dose would be between .25 and 1 gram of dried mushrooms. An average dosage would be between 1 gram and 2.5 grams of dried mushrooms. A strong dosage would be between 2.5 grams and 5 grams, with 3.5 grams being typical; 5 grams or more is considered to be a heavy or "heroic dose."

Note: reportedly, some individuals have gradually worked their way up to 30 grams and more, over time, without lasting ill effects.

The main psychoactive compound in psilocybin mushrooms, psilocybin, when chemically extracted is a white powder that can be taken orally, sniffed, smoked, or injected. Although psilocybin can be chemically extracted, for most people simply eating the dried mushroom or making a tea for consumption is sufficient. Dosages for the pure extract would be far lower than with dried mushrooms and are not included here.

SALVIA DIVINORUM

Salvia divinorum is the only psychoactive sage known to science. It is native to Oaxaca, Mexico, and is said to be a traditional sacred herb of the local Mazateca people, who use it for spiritual practices and healing.

The psychoactive compound in *Salvia divinorum* is Salvinorin A, which unlike most other psychedelics is not an alkaloid but is instead a diterpenoid. This molecular difference may be one reason that *Salvia divinorum* has yet to gain much legal attention.

Salvinorin A is the most powerful naturally occurring psychoactive substance known to science.

Effects

According to sagewisdom.org, with salvia there are various experiential possibilities depending upon dosage and individual sensitivities.

The most subtle effects are a relaxed, meditative state with enhanced sensual appreciation. Stronger effects may include enhanced color, texture, or increased or decreased depth to the visual field. Thinking becomes more open and less rigidly logical. Slightly more powerful trips can bring on dreamlike images and feelings similar to the hypnogogic state that occurs just before falling asleep. More powerful still are experiences of traveling to other lands, time-traveling, and even living other people's lives. These experiences can appear totally real to the individual. The most powerful salvia trips let the individual break through reality entirely to experience "The Source" or "Godhead." At this level one may merge with objects and become them, much like the way I became asphalt. Beyond this level of potency, the individual usually remembers nothing of the trip.

These stages quite accurately describe my own experiences with salvia.

When compared to ingesting psilocybin mushrooms or ayahuasca, salvia is a lot easier on the system, as there is no stomach upset, diarrhea, vomiting, sweats, chills, et cetera.

Regarding negative psychological effects, many people report unpleasant responses to high doses of salvia, such as terror and panic attacks, and because of the high potency of salvia, it is very easy to get an unexpectedly high dose by smoking or vaporizing it. Chewing salvia seems to offer a milder and more pleasant experience.

The biggest physical danger of salvia, by far, is your own panic to the overwhelming power of the experience. On high doses, people are apt to physically move about, which can cause injury. To counter the possibility of injury, have a helper watch over you.

My only aftereffect, if I could call it that, is that for about a week after my concentrated trips, I was somewhat spaced out and forgetful. It felt as if my brain was reorganizing itself in a positive way during this time. About a week after my last salvia trip, my mental focus and memory normalized.

The scant literature on *Salvia divinorum* says that it is nonaddictive and nontolerance-building. My experience with salvia seems to be a confirmation of both these factors. I tried it nine times over a period of two weeks and never experienced any reduction in potency, as one would with psilocybin. After the ninth trip, I knew I was done, and that was that. I had no compulsion to try it again.

After each session with salvia, my body quickly normalized, and I felt totally sober. Only after I had come to the conclusion to love and be happy regardless of circumstances did I notice a deep and lasting feeling of well-being that reached well past the completion of the trip. Unconditioned love and happiness are still, in fact, continuing.

Is my "wellness" a result of the chemical permanently altering my brain, or is it because of what I learned through the experience? Lacking any experimental studies to say one way or the other, who can say for sure?

Safety Profile

As of this writing there have been no safety studies on *Salvia divinorum* in humans.

A 2008 National Survey on Drug Use and Health (NSDUH) found that close to 2 million Americans had tried salvia, so we know that salvia is a very popular psychedelic.

Considering the numbers of people using salvia and the fact that not a single death has been attributed to salvia overdose, it would seem to be at least a relatively safe substance, assuming one has prepared the proper mindset and setting, but who knows what future studies will show?

Although no one has yet died from overdose, there have been a number of reports of people injuring themselves from apparent panic attacks while on salvia. It is important to note that many of the individuals who have injured themselves as a result of an apparent panic attack have no recollection of moving about.

Legality

Salvia divinorum is legal in most states and countries around the world. However, as of this writing, *Salvia divinorum* and Salvinorin A are controlled substances in Belgium, Denmark, Italy, Latvia, Lithuania, Romania, Sweden, Australia, and Japan. Numerous U.S. states and cities that have declared *Salvia divinorum* to be illegal, so any potential user would be well advised to check local legality before taking possession of the plant.

Where it is legal, salvia is commonly sold at smokeshops and headshops, and it is easily found online.

Method of Use

Traditionally, the Mazatec chewed and swallowed large quantities of the leaves over a period of about half an hour. Much of the psychoactive substance is absorbed through the mouth with this method, and some through the stomach. Consuming salvia in this way produces longer trips than does smoking.

Another traditional method is to grind up the leaves and steep them in water before drinking the liquid. Be warned that the leaves are reported to be quite unpalatable.

If one were inclined to chew salvia, then using it as a quid might be a more effective route. In the quid method, one would chew 2 to 8 grams of dried leaves, slowly, for a half hour, being careful to keep the mass under the tongue between the chews. The goal is keep the juice in the mouth for the allotted time before spitting out the quid.

As with eating the leaves, the quid method has a slower uptake but also longer peak duration. The full effects are likely to come on within 30 minutes, and the peak can last up to an hour or more.

By far, the most common and easiest way to take salvia is smoking the dried leaf. Salvia needs to burn hot, so a torch lighter and a water bong are good investments. The smoke needs to be inhaled quickly and deeply, which can be quite hard with the high temperatures that a torch lighter can generate. For this reason, having a pipe that will allow the smoke to cool before entering your body is a good idea.

The effects of salvia can come on so fast that you may unexpectedly lose bodily control and drop a hot pipe, something that happened to me on my second journey. Fortunately I was able to quickly wipe the carpet to crush out any embers. Such a danger is easily averted by having a helper present to take the pipe from you. I got around this issue by smoking above a table, so the pipe would land on a hard, safe surface if I dropped it.

The onset of salvia is quick and powerful when smoked, so you could find yourself launched into a visionary space in well under a minute. For most users, the peak will last about five minutes. With sensitive people like me, even with the smoking method peak effects can last up to an hour. The comedown period is generally less than a half hour.

Vaporization is another possible method, but a specially constructed vaporizer is required as marijuana vaporizers will not work with salvia.

Salvia can also be taken as a tincture, but again, making a salvia tincture requires know-how, skill, and time that most people don't have. As of this writing tinctures can be purchased online. The benefit of taking salvia as a tincture is that the peak experience is greatly lengthened from just a few minutes when smoked to as much as an hour with the tincture.

For more information on *Salvia divinorum*, I highly recommend visiting sagewisdom.org, which has an excellent user guide, plus well-maintained and up-to-date scientific and legal information on *Salvia divinorum*.

Research Studies

Acute Physiologic and Chronic Histologic Changes in Rats and Mice Exposed to the Unique Hallucinogen Salvinorin A

In 2003 M. Mowry et al. published a study in the *Journal of Psychoactive Drugs* that concluded "acute administration of Salvinorin A had little discernable effect on the cardiovascular function of rats, with the exception of potential increases in pulse pressure. Its long term administration in mice failed to produce detectable histologic changes. This suggests that Salvinorin A, while a potent hallucinogen, has relatively low toxicity."

A Survey of *Salvia Divinorum* Users

In 2004 Matthew Baggot, with E. & F. Erowid, conducted a survey of 500 *Salvia divinorum* users who reported the following lingering effects after main salvia intoxication (numbers represent the percentage of users in the study who experienced the specified effect):

- Increased Insight   47.0
- Improved Mood   44.8
- Calmness   42.2
- Increased Connection with Universe or Nature

39.8

- Weird Thoughts   36.4
- Things Seem Unreal   32.4
- Floating Feeling   32.0
- Increased Sweating   28.2
- Body Felt Warm or Hot   25.2
- Mind Racing   23.2
- Lightheaded   22.2
- Increased Self-confidence   21.6
- Improved Concentration   19.4
- Drowsiness   18.8
- Dizziness   18.6
- Lack of Coordination   18.0
- Feel Like Someone or Something Else   14.0
- Heart Racing   13.2
- Bothered by Noises   12.2
- Difficulty Concentrating   12.0
- Yawning   11.8
- Anxiety   9.4
- Difficulty Sleeping   7.8
- Chills or Gooseflesh   7.0
- Increased Urine Production   6.4
- Body Felt Cold   6.4
- Watery Eyes   5.4
- Decreased Connection with Universe or Nature   5.4
- Irritable   5.0
- Worsened Mood   4.0
- Decreased Self-confidence   2.4

- Nausea 1.8
- Runny Nose or Sneezing 1.8
- Muscle Cramps or Aches 1.8
- Decreased Insight 1.8
- Decreased Sweating 1.6
- Decreased Urine Production 0.6
- Diarrhea 0.2
- Vomiting 0.0

In the same survey, *Salvia divinorum* was compared with other methods of altering consciousness (again, numbers represent the percentage of users in the study who experienced the specified effect.)

- SD is unique 38.4
- SD is like meditation/yoga/trances 23.2
- SD is like serotonergic hallucinogens (e.g., LSD) 17.7
- SD is like dreaming 7.1
- SD is like NMDA antagonists (e.g., ketamine) and other anesthetics 6.8
- SD is like cannabis 6.5

Final Thoughts on *Salvia Divinorum*, Psilocybin, and Ayahuasca:

When compared to psilocybin mushrooms or ayahuasca, *Salvia divinorum* effects seem to be much easier on the body. Salvia provides a quick uptake, shorter trips, and quicker comedowns. Also, both psilocybin mushrooms and ayahuasca can cause a hangover effect, whereas with salvia, hangover reports are rare, so taking salvia may seem an easy choice. Just remember that in the process of spiritual awakening, the pull leads where it leads, which is not always to convenience.

Consider that ayahuasca, psilocybin, and *Salvia divinorum* are distinct psychedelics that produce distinct experiences for most people. Furthermore, each person and each day is unique, so results can vary tremendously from trip to trip, even if one is using the same substance.

Another thing to consider with psychedelics is whether they provide a teaching element. Users commonly report meeting teacher entities while on ayahuasca and psilocybin, who serve to instruct them towards correcting their lives. One complaint that my students had when comparing salvia to psilocybin was that salvia seems to have no teaching element. Another complaint they had was about the incredibly short trips that smoked salvia affords. Because the trips are so short, there is very little ability to acclimate within the trip enough for much learning to occur. Taking salvia as a quid or tincture may be more suitable for people wishing to learn more from the trip.

Finally, I would like to remind the reader that these substances are not toys to be played with. An ayahuasca, psilocybin, or salvia trip could easily be the worst experience of your life—by far. I can't imagine using these substances to party. I have seen a few videos on YouTube of teens doing exactly that with *Salvia divinorum*. The results are less than inspiring.

People get hurt when they disrespect these powerful substances. Kids will be kids, so there may be no way to stop them from playing with psychedelics in a culture that lacks respect for psychedelics. Making psychedelics illegal has arguably done little or nothing to stop irresponsible, disrespecting individuals from playing with psychedelic fire, after all.

One of the benefits of learning from ayahuasca, *Salvia divinorum*, and psilocybin mushrooms is that the experiences contain sufficiently unpleasant aspects to curb irresponsible usage with most people after the first trip.

For your free 13-part audio series "Taking Spiritual Authority in Daily Life" by Richard L. Haight, visit: *www.richardhaight.net*

Glossary

Alkaloid *any of numerous usually colorless, complex, and bitter organic bases (such as morphine or caffeine) containing nitrogen and usually oxygen that occur especially in seed plants and are typically physiologically active.*

Acid *a street name for LSD (Lysergic acid diethylamide), a synthetic psychedelic drug.*

Ayahuasca *a hallucinogenic beverage prepared from the bark of a South American woody vine Banisteriopsis caapi.*

DMT *Dimethyltryptamine is a psychoactive tryptamine molecule which occurs in many plants and animals.*

Entheogen *Entheogen means "generating the divine within" and refers to any substance used in a religious, shamanic, or spiritual context that produces altered states of consciousness.*

Hallucinogen *a substance that induces hallucinations.*

Neuromodulators *substances, such as hormones, that influence the function of neurons but do not act as neurotransmitters.*

Neurotransmitters substances that transmit nerve impulses across a synapse.

Psychedelic drug *a psychoactive chemical that alters cognition and perception, such as LSD, psilocybin mushrooms, mescaline, and DMT.*

Psychoactive *affecting the mind or behavior.*

Psychotropic *substances that act on the mind.*

Psilocybin *a psychedelic alkaloid obtained from mushrooms such as Psilocybe cubensis.*

Psilocin *a psychedelic alkaloid obtained from mushrooms such as Psilocybe cubensis.*

Salvia *any of a large and widely distributed genus of herbs and shrubs of the mint family.*

Salvia Divinorum *a plant species native to Mexico with psychoactive properties.*

Salvinorin A *the main active psychotropic molecule in Salvia divinorum.*

Shaman *a priest or priestess who uses altered states of consciousness in order to perceive and interact with a spirit world, heal, and find wisdom.*

Tryptamines *a set of biologically active compounds found in many flora and fauna around the world. Tryptamines are hypothesized to play a role as a neuromodulator or neurotransmitter. Most psychedelic substances are tryptamines.*

Resources

Here are a few great sources for anyone who is looking for quality information on psychedelics.

MAPS
Multidisciplinary Association for Psychedelic Studies. MAPS is a 501(c)(3) non-profit research and educational organization that develops medical, legal, and cultural contexts for people to benefit from the careful uses of psychedelics and marijuana.
maps.org

HEFFTER RESEARCH INSTITUTE
Advancing studies on psilocybin for cancer distress and addiction with the highest standards of scientific research

EROWID
Documenting the Complex Relationship between Humans & Psychedelics
erowid.org

Sage Wisdom
The Salvia divinorum Research and Information Center
sagewisdom.org

About the Author

Richard L. Haight is an instructor of martial, meditation, and healing arts, and he is the author of *The Unbound Soul: A Spiritual Memoir for Personal Transformation and Enlightenment.*

He began his path of awakening at age eight when he made a solemn promise in a vision to dedicate his life to enlightenment and to share what he found with the world. He took his first steps towards that promise at age 12 when he began formal martial arts training.

At the age of 24, Richard moved to Japan to advance his training with masters of the sword, staff, and aiki-jujutsu. During his 15 years living in Japan, Richard was awarded masters licenses in four samurai arts as well as a traditional healing art called Sotai-ho.

Throughout his life, Richard has had a series of profound visions that have ultimately guided him to the realization of the Oneness that the ancient spiritual teachers often spoke of. This understanding ultimately transformed the arts that he teaches and has resulted in the writing of *The Unbound Soul.*

Through his books, his meditation and martial arts seminar, Richard Haight is helping to ignite a worldwide spiritual awakening that is free of all constraints and open to anyone of any level. Richard Haight now lives and teaches in southern Oregon, U.S.A.

Richard Haight explains that true spiritual enlightenment embraces all of life with deep aliveness, authenticity, innocence and authority. It is what you are truly seeking.

The Unbound Soul

*A Spiritual Memoir for Personal
Transformation and Enlightenment*

The heartfelt, true story of a young boy, who, in the midst of a vision, dedicates his life to spiritual awakening. As he matures into a man, this promise leads him across the globe, gathering ancient knowledge and mastering martial, healing, and meditation arts. Along the way, subsequent visions reveal the rapidly approaching collapse that will shake our societies, our economic system, and the earth's ecology to the very core. Tormented by visions of coming worldwide calamity, he presses ever onward in his search and eventually realizes the elusive truth hinted at in his childhood vision. In *The Unbound Soul*, Haight reveals the profoundly simple yet elusive truth that illuminates your life. *The Unbound Soul* is really about you and your path toward practical realization in everyday life.

"This is a must read for anyone searching to explore

spirituality, purpose, and unbound freedom."
—*Greg Giesen, Award-winning author of Monday at 3 and Creating Authenticity*

Through this work, among other things, you will:

- Receive new tools of awakening that blend seamlessly into your daily life. — *"This book is worth getting just for this, but it's a whole lot more."*
- Learn how the senses, thought, emotion and memory have imprisoned you, and discover the key to unlocking that prison. — *"...one of the most profound books I've read in the search for answers to Love, Life, and Living!"*
- Discover the nature of the mind, consciousness, the spirit and the soul, and how they interweave to limit or unleash the possibilities of your daily experience. — *"You will look at the world a little bit differently after reading it."*
- Learn how to turn your daily life into a vibrant journey of awakening. — *"No gimmicks. No special pictures or runes. JUST YOU."*

"Any reader who likes to contemplate and seek the ultimate truth will not turn away from this book once he or she picks it up!"

"This book, in my humble opinion, is the best literary tool for all human souls seeking their inner path to 'Spiritual Unfoldment.'"

"If you feel any drawing to read this book, know that it has the potential to transform your life."

Inspirience
Meditation Unbound
The Unconditioned Path to Spiritual Awakening

"I read one spiritual book a week for my radio show, and I will tell you that *Inspirience is fresh, genuine, and much needed!"* --*Jean Adrienne, PowerTalk Radio*

EXPERIENCING LIFE

INSPIRING CHANGE

LIVING INSPIRIENCE

What is it you truly seek? The reality is, most of us don't really know. Upon close investigation, we discover, above all else, we are seeking the transcendent, that which resides at the deepest place within us, that which connects us to all that is and gives unconditioned meaning to our lives.

The transcendent exceeds the grasp of the mind and the limits of words, for it is beyond all form and definition. But inspirience, although it cannot be explained in words, can be found. There is a path to it.

Richard L. Haight, the bestselling author of The Unbound Soul, master meditator and swordsman, shares a simple and natural way to inspirience through unconditioned meditation. Inspirience will take you on a journey to the transcendent, so that it can transform your life--and the world.

- Learn the essence of meditation and be free of complications, traditions, and dogma. — *"Astonishingly practical...without dogma, without unattainable requirements of countless hours of practice and study."*
- Transform meditation it into a powerful guidance system for your daily life and spiritual path. — *"The different meditations he teaches...seem to give me a deeper connection to All That Is."*
- Learn how meditation can clear your inner deadwood and correct your life-pattern, so you can move forward, heart as light as a feather. — *"He gets us to the point where we can be comfortable with our inner space, who we are and confront aspects of the self that we don't like."*
- Learn how to bring true purpose and meaning into your life and thereby transcend the lurking feelings of frustration, emptiness, and loneliness. — *"He provides clear, simple yet profound guidelines on conscious living, meditation, and the path as one goes about daily living."*

"A short, easy, fun read. To say that I find this book highly useful and refreshing would be an

understatement."

"He has this straight-forward approach that gives a feeling of utter confidence in him."

"Wonderfully down to earth, easy to understand and full of his own experiences and explorations which are absolute treasures."

Coming Soon...

Dance of the Self

Moving Beyond Suffering

For more information visit:
www.richardhaight.net

Made in the
USA
Columbia, SC